THE

HINDENBURG

DISASTER

Complete History

By

History Horizon

PREFACE

The name "Hindenburg" evokes a singular image in history—an awe-inspiring marvel of engineering engulfed in flames as it descended from the skies on May 6, 1937. This moment, frozen in time by haunting photographs, eyewitness accounts, and the infamous radio broadcast, marked not just the tragic end of an airship but the demise of an entire era of aviation.

This book, *The Hindenburg Disaster: Complete History*, delves beyond the sensational headlines to explore the story of a vessel that once represented the pinnacle of human ingenuity. The Hindenburg was not merely an airship; it was a floating palace that symbolized progress, luxury, and ambition. Yet, in its fiery end, it became a symbol of technological vulnerability and the high cost of overconfidence.

In these pages, we trace the Hindenburg's journey from its conception to its catastrophic conclusion. We explore the context of its time, when airships promised to redefine travel, and examine the sequence of events that culminated in one of the most infamous disasters in aviation history. Through a meticulous investigation of the facts, theories, and aftermath, this book aims to honor those who perished, illuminate the lessons learned, and preserve the legacy of the Hindenburg for generations to come.

The Hindenburg disaster was more than a singular tragedy; it was a turning point in the history of aviation, a sobering reminder of the fragility of human ambition, and a testament to the resilience of those who survived. As we recount this remarkable story, we invite readers to step back in time, to marvel at the audacity of those who dared to dream of conquering the skies, and to reflect on the enduring impact of that fateful day.

History has many lessons to teach, and the Hindenburg's story is one of them—a tale of innovation, risk, and the pursuit of progress, often at a cost. May this book not only educate but also inspire reflection on the remarkable journey of human ingenuity and the lessons we carry forward from our past.

History Horizon

Table of Contents

Introduction: The Rise and Fall of the Hindenburg

- o Overview of the Hindenburg disaster and its significance in aviation history.

Chapter 1: The Age of Airships

- o The history of airship travel before the Hindenburg.

- o The development of the LZ 129 Hindenburg.

- o The role of German Zeppelin Company in shaping airship technology.

Chapter 2: The Hindenburg – A Marvel of Engineering

- o Construction and design of the Hindenburg.

- o Features and specifications that made it a symbol of luxury and progress.

Chapter 3: The Hindenburg's Maiden Voyage and Successes

- o First flight and the journey to fame.

- o The Hindenburg's role in transatlantic travel and public perception.

Chapter 4: The Fateful Flight – May 6, 1937

- o The journey from Frankfurt to Lakehurst, New Jersey.

- Conditions leading up to the disaster.
- Key figures on board.

Chapter 5: The Hindenburg Disaster

- Step-by-step account of the explosion and crash.
- Eyewitness testimonies and radio broadcasts.
- Immediate aftermath and the chaotic rescue efforts.

Chapter 6: Causes of the Hindenburg Disaster

- Investigation into the cause of the fire.
- Theories: hydrogen vs. static electricity, sabotage, and others.
- Insights from engineers and experts.

Chapter 7: The Hindenburg's Impact on Air Travel

- How the disaster changed public opinion about airships.
- The decline of airship travel and rise of airplanes.
- Lasting changes in aviation safety standards.

Chapter 8: The Legacy of the Hindenburg

- The enduring image of the Hindenburg in popular culture.
- The survivors and their lives after the crash.
- Memorials and honors for those who perished.

Chapter 9: Reassessing the Disaster: Myths vs. Facts

- Debunking common myths surrounding the Hindenburg disaster.
- Modern perspectives on the tragedy.

2. **Conclusion: Lessons Learned and the End of the Airship Era**

    - Reflections on the Hindenburg's place in history.
    - The broader lessons for aviation and technology.

INTRODUCTION

The Rise and Fall of the Hindenburg

On the evening of May 6, 1937, the skies above Lakehurst, New Jersey, bore witness to one of the most infamous tragedies in aviation history. The German airship LZ 129 Hindenburg, once a beacon of technological prowess and luxury, was consumed by flames as it attempted to dock. In just 37 seconds, the majestic zeppelin was reduced to a smoldering wreck, leaving 36 people dead and the world in shock.

The Hindenburg disaster marked the end of an era—the golden age of airships. For nearly four decades, zeppelins had captured the imagination of the public, offering a glimpse into the future of air travel. These giant vessels, gracefully gliding through the skies, promised not only speed and efficiency but also opulence and grandeur. Among them, the Hindenburg was the crown jewel—a symbol of progress, engineering ingenuity, and German pride.

Built by the Zeppelin Company, the Hindenburg was the largest airship ever constructed, measuring over 800 feet in length. Its size, elegance, and ability to cross the Atlantic in record time made it a marvel of its age. Equipped with a dining room, smoking lounge, and private cabins, it catered to the elite, offering an experience akin to a luxury cruise in the skies. However, the same innovation that made the Hindenburg extraordinary also carried inherent risks.

The disaster's impact was far-reaching, not only because of its dramatic nature but also due to its timing. The 1930s were a period of rapid technological advancement, and airships had been poised to revolutionize global travel. Yet, the Hindenburg's fiery end abruptly shattered public confidence in the safety of lighter-than-air travel. The event signaled the decline of airships and the rise of airplanes, which would go on to dominate the aviation industry.

The significance of the Hindenburg disaster lies not only in its tragic loss of life but also in its symbolic resonance. It was a cautionary tale about the perils of innovation without sufficient safeguards. The use of hydrogen, a highly flammable gas, was a calculated risk, driven in part by political and economic pressures. This choice would prove catastrophic, as the gas fueled the fire that engulfed the airship.

The Hindenburg's story is also a testament to the resilience of the human spirit. Despite the chaos and devastation, many passengers and crew members survived, thanks to the heroic efforts of rescuers and the quick thinking of those aboard. Their accounts provide invaluable insights into the events of that fateful day, as well as the airship's final moments.

This introduction sets the stage for an in-depth exploration of the Hindenburg's rise and fall. From its conception and construction to its tragic demise and enduring legacy, the chapters that follow aim to unravel the complexities of this extraordinary story. By examining the Hindenburg's place in history, we can better understand the interplay between ambition, technology, and human fallibility—a dynamic that continues to shape the trajectory of progress.

The Hindenburg was more than an airship; it was a symbol of its time. Its rise reflected humanity's unyielding desire to innovate and explore, while its fall served as a sobering reminder of the consequences of underestimating risk. In the end, the Hindenburg disaster was not just a moment in history but a turning point that redefined the course of aviation and left an indelible mark on the collective consciousness of the modern world.

CHAPTER 1

THE AGE OF AIRSHIPS

Before the Hindenburg captured the world's attention with its catastrophic end, airships had been symbols of human ingenuity and a testament to the relentless pursuit of innovation. For decades, these massive, lighter-than-air vessels were the pinnacle of aviation technology, inspiring awe as they glided silently across the skies. The age of airships, beginning in the late 19th century and flourishing in the early 20th century, was marked by both triumphs and tragedies, reflecting humanity's desire to conquer the heavens.

The Origins of Airships

The concept of airships dates back to the late 18th century, following the invention of the hot air balloon by the Montgolfier brothers in 1783. While balloons could ascend and drift with the wind, they lacked navigational control. This limitation spurred inventors to develop a means of steering and propelling such airborne vessels. The introduction of the cigar-shaped, powered airship in the mid-19th century marked the dawn of the dirigible era.

In 1852, French engineer Henri Giffard built the first successful airship, powered by a small steam engine. Though slow and cumbersome, Giffard's dirigible proved that controlled flight was possible. Over the following decades, technological advancements in engines, materials, and design led to significant improvements in speed, maneuverability, and range, paving the way for the age of airships.

The Zeppelin Revolution

The true breakthrough in airship design came with the work of Count Ferdinand von Zeppelin. A former German army officer, Zeppelin envisioned a rigid, frame-based airship that could carry passengers and cargo over long distances. In 1900, the first Zeppelin, LZ 1, made its maiden flight over Lake Constance in Germany. Though the flight lasted only 18 minutes, it marked the beginning of a new era in aviation.

Zeppelins were characterized by their rigid aluminum frames, which were covered with fabric and contained multiple gas cells filled with hydrogen or helium. This design provided structural stability and allowed for larger vessels capable of carrying more passengers and cargo. Zeppelin's subsequent models, such as the LZ 3 and LZ 4, demonstrated remarkable endurance and reliability, earning the support of the German government and the public.

By the early 20th century, zeppelins had become a fixture in the skies, used for both civilian and military purposes. During World War I, Germany deployed zeppelins as bombers and reconnaissance vehicles, though their vulnerability to enemy fire limited their effectiveness. Despite these setbacks, the war years solidified the Zeppelin Company's reputation as a leader in airship technology.

The Golden Age of Airships

The 1920s and 1930s marked the golden age of airships, as advancements in engineering and materials made them larger, faster, and more luxurious. These years saw the rise of passenger airships, which offered unparalleled comfort and elegance. Wealthy travelers could enjoy spacious cabins, fine dining, and scenic views while crossing oceans in style.

Among the most notable airships of this era was the British R101, which was designed to connect Britain's far-flung empire. Though the R101 met a tragic end in 1930, its construction showcased the ambition and technological prowess of the time.

In the United States, the U.S. Navy developed a series of rigid airships, including the USS Akron and USS Macon, which served as flying aircraft carriers. These vessels demonstrated the versatility of airships, though their operational challenges highlighted the risks inherent in lighter-than-air travel.

The Rise of the Hindenburg

By the mid-1930s, airships were at the height of their popularity, and the Zeppelin Company's LZ 129 Hindenburg represented the pinnacle of this technology. Larger and more advanced than any airship before it, the Hindenburg was a testament to the progress achieved during the age of airships. It was designed to provide a fast and luxurious transatlantic travel experience, bridging continents with unparalleled efficiency.

However, the golden age of airships was already under threat. The development of heavier-than-air craft, particularly airplanes, posed a formidable challenge to the dominance of airships. While airplanes were smaller and less comfortable, they were faster, more versatile, and less reliant on the unpredictable behavior of lighter-than-air gases.

Triumphs and Tragedies

The age of airships was marked by extraordinary achievements, but it was also fraught with peril. The reliance on hydrogen, a highly flammable gas, contributed to several high-profile disasters, such as the explosion of the French airship Dixmude in 1923 and the loss of the British R101. These incidents underscored the inherent risks of airship travel, even as advancements continued to improve safety and reliability.

The Hindenburg disaster of 1937 would ultimately seal the fate of airships. While it was not the first tragedy of its kind, its dramatic and highly publicized nature struck a fatal blow to the public's confidence in lighter-than-air travel. Within a few years, airships were largely relegated to niche roles, such as advertising and sightseeing, as airplanes became the dominant mode of air travel.

Legacy of the Age of Airships

The age of airships was a unique chapter in the history of aviation, marked by bold innovation, breathtaking ambition, and profound challenges. These majestic vessels captured the imagination of the world, symbolizing both the heights of human ingenuity and the dangers of pushing boundaries without fully understanding the risks.

Today, airships remain a source of fascination and nostalgia. Their legacy endures in modern aviation, where lessons from their triumphs and tragedies continue to inform the pursuit of safer and more efficient technologies. As we reflect on this bygone era, we are reminded of the enduring human spirit that dared to dream of conquering the skies, even when the odds were daunting.

The Hindenburg was the final chapter in this remarkable story—a crowning achievement and a tragic conclusion to an age defined by its pursuit of the extraordinary.

The Development of the LZ 129 Hindenburg

The LZ 129 Hindenburg was not merely an airship; it was a masterpiece of engineering and a symbol of human ambition during the interwar years. Conceived as the pinnacle of Zeppelin technology, it embodied the aspirations of an era striving to conquer the skies with grandeur and efficiency. Its development was a complex process shaped by technological innovations, political influences, and a vision of redefining transatlantic travel.

Vision and Ambition

The Zeppelin Company, under the leadership of Hugo Eckener, envisioned the LZ 129 as a revolutionary airship. Following the success of earlier models such as the LZ 127 Graf Zeppelin, which completed a record-breaking global voyage in 1929, the company sought to build an airship that would cement its dominance in long-distance air travel.

The Hindenburg was designed to be the largest airship ever constructed, with a length of 804 feet and a diameter of 135 feet. It would surpass all predecessors in size, capacity, and speed, offering luxurious accommodations for passengers traveling across the Atlantic. The Zeppelin Company aimed to attract wealthy clientele, making the Hindenburg not just a mode of transportation but a statement of luxury and modernity.

Technological Innovation

The construction of the Hindenburg represented a culmination of decades of experience in airship engineering. Its rigid framework was made from duralumin, a lightweight and strong aluminum alloy. The internal structure housed 16 gas cells, each made of cotton fabric coated with gelatinized latex to hold the lifting gas.

Originally, the Hindenburg was intended to use helium, a non-flammable and safer gas than hydrogen. However, due to geopolitical constraints—specifically the U.S. monopoly on helium and its embargo on exports to Germany—the Zeppelin Company was forced to use hydrogen. This decision introduced significant risks, as hydrogen is highly flammable and had contributed to earlier airship disasters.

To power the Hindenburg, four Daimler-Benz DB 602 diesel engines were installed, each capable of producing 1,200 horsepower. These engines allowed the airship to reach a maximum speed of 84 miles per hour, making it one of the fastest airships of its time. Additionally, its cruising range of over 8,000 miles enabled nonstop transatlantic crossings, a major selling point for passengers seeking efficiency.

Design and Luxury

The Hindenburg was not just a feat of engineering; it was also a marvel of design. The interior, designed by German architect Fritz August Breuhaus, featured Art Deco aesthetics and catered to the comfort of its passengers. The ship could accommodate up to 72 passengers in private cabins, each equipped with a sink and foldable bed. Public spaces included a dining room, a lounge with a grand piano, and a smoking room—a surprising addition given the presence of hydrogen, though it was carefully engineered to prevent accidents.

Passengers enjoyed gourmet meals prepared in a fully equipped kitchen, as well as panoramic views of the Earth from observation windows. This combination of luxury and innovation made the Hindenburg a floating palace in the sky, unrivaled by any other mode of travel at the time.

Political and Economic Factors

The development of the Hindenburg was not just a commercial endeavor; it was also influenced by the political and economic landscape of 1930s Germany. The Zeppelin Company received substantial support from the Nazi regime, which saw the airship as a propaganda tool to showcase German technological superiority. The Hindenburg's maiden flight in 1936 was heavily promoted, with swastikas emblazoned on its tail fins, reinforcing its role as a symbol of national pride.

Economic challenges also played a role in the ship's development. The Great Depression had strained the finances of the Zeppelin Company, and attracting wealthy passengers became critical to its success. The luxurious design of the Hindenburg was as much about creating a competitive edge as it was about meeting the expectations of its clientele.

Testing and Maiden Voyage

Construction of the Hindenburg began in 1931 at the Zeppelin Company's hangar in Friedrichshafen, Germany, and was completed in 1936. Before its public debut, the airship underwent rigorous testing to ensure its safety and performance. Engineers and crew members conducted trial flights, fine-tuning its systems and addressing any potential issues.

The Hindenburg's maiden voyage took place on March 4, 1936, marking the beginning of its operational career. It quickly gained fame for its smooth, efficient, and luxurious service. Over the course of 1936, it completed 17 transatlantic flights, transporting passengers and mail between Germany and the United States. These flights solidified its reputation as a technological marvel and an icon of the golden age of airships.

The Legacy of Its Development

The development of the LZ 129 Hindenburg was a bold venture that pushed the boundaries of what was possible in aviation during its time. It represented the pinnacle of Zeppelin technology, combining innovation, luxury, and ambition in a single vessel. However, the compromises made during its construction—particularly the use of hydrogen— ultimately sealed its fate.

The Hindenburg was not just an airship; it was a symbol of its era, embodying the triumphs and challenges of human ingenuity. Its development remains a testament to the audacity of visionaries who dared to dream of a future where the skies were no longer a limit but a pathway to new possibilities. While its end would overshadow its achievements, the story of the Hindenburg's creation continues to inspire and caution those who seek to innovate and explore the unknown.

The Role of the German Zeppelin Company in Shaping Airship Technology

The story of airships is inseparable from the legacy of the German Zeppelin Company, which not only pioneered advancements in lighter-than-air flight but also became synonymous with luxury, innovation, and ambition. Founded at the turn of the 20th century, the company transformed airships from experimental novelties into practical and sophisticated modes of transportation. Through technological breakthroughs, bold design choices, and strategic leadership, the Zeppelin Company played a pivotal role in shaping the golden age of airships.

The Visionary Founding

The German Zeppelin Company, formally known as Luftschiffbau Zeppelin GmbH, was established in 1908 by Count Ferdinand von Zeppelin. Count Zeppelin, a former military officer, became fascinated with aviation after witnessing a tethered balloon flight during the American Civil War. Convinced of the potential for airships to revolutionize transportation and military strategy, he dedicated himself to their development.

Count Zeppelin envisioned a rigid airship that could overcome the limitations of earlier designs. Unlike non-rigid or semi-rigid airships, which relied on their outer envelope for structural integrity, rigid airships utilized a lightweight but durable framework to maintain their shape. This innovation allowed for larger, more stable vessels capable of carrying significant payloads over long distances.

The company's first prototype, the LZ 1, took flight on July 2, 1900, over Lake Constance. Though its maiden voyage was brief and marked by mechanical issues, it demonstrated the potential of rigid airships and laid the foundation for future advancements.

Early Challenges and Triumphs

The Zeppelin Company faced significant challenges in its early years, including financial difficulties and skepticism from the public and investors. The initial airships suffered from technical limitations and occasional crashes, fueling doubts about their viability.

However, Count Zeppelin's perseverance and the company's commitment to innovation gradually won over critics. The LZ 3, introduced in 1906, became the first Zeppelin to achieve commercial success, demonstrating reliability and endurance in a series of public flights. By the early 1910s, the company had established itself as a leader in airship technology, producing models like the LZ 10 Schwaben, which offered passenger services and garnered widespread acclaim.

Military Applications

The Zeppelin Company's prominence grew during World War I, when Germany recognized the strategic potential of airships for reconnaissance, bombing, and propaganda missions. The company produced a fleet of military Zeppelins that played a pivotal role in the war effort.

Zeppelins were used for long-range bombing raids over Britain, targeting cities like London and causing widespread alarm. Although their effectiveness as bombers was limited by their vulnerability to anti-aircraft fire and unpredictable weather, they excelled in reconnaissance, providing valuable intelligence to German forces.

The war years solidified the Zeppelin Company's reputation for technological expertise, even as the military use of airships exposed their limitations. Despite setbacks, including the loss of several airships to enemy fire, the company's innovations during this period advanced the field of aviation.

The Post-War Revival

The Treaty of Versailles imposed strict limitations on Germany's aviation industry, temporarily halting the production of Zeppelins. However, the Zeppelin Company made a remarkable comeback in the 1920s under the leadership of Hugo Eckener, a close associate of Count Zeppelin.

Eckener shifted the company's focus from military applications to civilian air travel, envisioning airships as a luxurious and efficient means of long-distance transportation. This pivot led to the creation of the LZ 127 Graf Zeppelin, which became an international sensation.

Launched in 1928, the Graf Zeppelin completed numerous record-breaking flights, including a historic circumnavigation of the globe in 1929. These achievements showcased the potential of airships for peaceful purposes, earning the Zeppelin Company global acclaim and restoring its financial stability.

The Pinnacle of Innovation: The Hindenburg

The Zeppelin Company's crowning achievement came with the development of the LZ 129 Hindenburg, the largest and most advanced airship ever built. Designed to offer luxurious transatlantic travel, the Hindenburg represented the culmination of decades of expertise in airship engineering.

The Hindenburg's success in 1936, completing 17 transatlantic crossings, demonstrated the company's ability to deliver on its promise of reliable, high-speed travel. However, the tragic disaster of 1937 overshadowed its achievements and marked the beginning of the end for the Zeppelin Company's dominance in aviation.

Legacy and Influence

The Zeppelin Company's contributions to airship technology extended far beyond its own designs. Many of the principles it developed—such as the use of rigid frameworks, advancements in aerodynamics, and innovations in lightweight materials—influenced subsequent generations of aircraft and even spacecraft.

The company's focus on safety, reliability, and passenger comfort also set a standard for modern aviation. Its commitment to luxury and elegance, exemplified by the Graf Zeppelin and the Hindenburg, left an indelible mark on the history of transportation.

Challenges and Decline

Despite its achievements, the Zeppelin Company faced insurmountable challenges as airplanes emerged as a more practical and versatile alternative to airships. The Hindenburg disaster dealt a severe blow to public confidence in airships, and advancements in heavier-than-air technology rendered them increasingly obsolete.

The outbreak of World War II further curtailed the production and use of airships, as Germany shifted its focus to airplanes and other military technologies. By the mid-20th century, the Zeppelin Company had largely ceased operations, leaving behind a legacy of innovation and ambition.

Conclusion

The German Zeppelin Company played a central role in shaping the development of airship technology, transforming it from a fledgling concept into a symbol of human ingenuity. Its achievements in engineering, design, and aviation strategy paved the way for the golden age of airships and inspired countless innovations in the field of aviation.

Though the age of Zeppelins has long passed, the company's legacy endures as a testament to the power of vision, perseverance, and the relentless pursuit of progress. The story of the Zeppelin Company is not just about airships; it is about the human spirit's capacity to dream and achieve the extraordinary.

CHAPTER 2

THE HINDENBURG – A MARVEL OF ENGINEERING

The LZ 129 Hindenburg, an engineering masterpiece of its time, symbolized the pinnacle of airship technology. Designed to provide luxurious, efficient, and long-range air travel, the Hindenburg was not only a marvel of design but also a testament to human ambition and ingenuity. This chapter explores the construction and design of the Hindenburg, highlighting the innovations that made it the largest and most advanced airship ever built.

The Conception of the Hindenburg

The idea for the Hindenburg emerged during the 1930s, a period when airships represented the height of technological sophistication. The German Zeppelin Company sought to build an airship capable of revolutionizing transatlantic travel, offering a faster and more comfortable alternative to ocean liners.

Named after Paul von Hindenburg, a former president of Germany, the airship was conceived as a symbol of German engineering prowess and a tool to restore national pride during a turbulent time in the country's history.

Construction of the Hindenburg began in 1931 under the leadership of Hugo Eckener, the director of the Zeppelin Company, and Ludwig Dürr, the chief engineer. The project combined advanced materials, meticulous design, and cutting-edge aerodynamics to create an airship of unparalleled size and capability.

Dimensions and Structure

At 245 meters (804 feet) long and 41.2 meters (135 feet) in diameter, the Hindenburg was the largest aircraft ever built. Its immense size dwarfed contemporary airplanes and even most modern ones, underscoring the scale of its ambition.

The Hindenburg featured a rigid framework made of duralumin, a lightweight and strong aluminum alloy. This framework was composed of 15 main ring girders and longitudinal girders, which created a lattice structure capable of withstanding the stresses of flight. The outer covering, made of cotton fabric coated with a cellulose acetate solution, provided weather resistance and aerodynamic smoothness.

Gas Cells and Lift

The airship's lift was generated by 16 gas cells housed within its framework. These cells were made of gelatinized cotton and held hydrogen, a highly flammable gas but one that was chosen due to its availability and superior lifting properties compared to helium.

The decision to use hydrogen was a compromise forced by geopolitical realities. The United States, the primary supplier of helium, restricted its export due to political tensions and concerns about its use in German military applications. Despite hydrogen's risks, the Zeppelin Company employed advanced safety measures to mitigate the dangers.

Propulsion and Performance

The Hindenburg was powered by four Daimler-Benz DB 602 diesel engines, each capable of producing 1,200 horsepower. These engines were chosen for their reliability, fuel efficiency, and ability to operate for extended periods without overheating.

With a cruising speed of 125 km/h (78 mph) and a maximum speed of 135 km/h (84 mph), the Hindenburg was among the fastest airships of its era. It could carry up to 72 passengers and 61 crew members on long-distance journeys, including transatlantic crossings in just two to three days—far faster than ocean liners.

Luxurious Interiors

The Hindenburg was designed not only for efficiency but also for elegance. Its passenger accommodations rivaled those of the finest ocean liners, offering an unparalleled level of comfort and luxury in the skies.

The main passenger deck, known as the "A Deck," featured a dining room, lounge, writing room, and promenade with panoramic windows. The interior decor was minimalist yet sophisticated, with lightweight materials used to balance aesthetics with functionality.

The lounge contained a grand piano made of aluminum to reduce weight, and the walls were adorned with a mural depicting the Graf Zeppelin's flight over the Arctic. Sleeping quarters included double and single cabins, each equipped with washbasins and foldable beds to maximize space.

Innovations in Safety and Design

The Zeppelin Company incorporated numerous safety features into the Hindenburg's design to address the inherent risks of hydrogen. These included:

- **Fireproof bulkheads** separating the gas cells.

- **Automatic gas valves** to relieve pressure and prevent ruptures.

- **State-of-the-art materials** designed to minimize the risk of sparks and static discharge.

Despite these measures, the use of hydrogen remained the airship's greatest vulnerability—a fact that would later contribute to its tragic fate.

Navigational Systems

The Hindenburg was equipped with advanced navigational instruments for its time, including altimeters, compasses, and radio equipment. The control car, located beneath the nose of the airship, served as the operational hub for navigation, communication, and flight control.

The airship also featured an innovative ballast system to maintain stability during flight. Water ballast tanks allowed for precise adjustments to the ship's weight and balance, ensuring smooth handling even in turbulent weather.

The Maiden Voyage

The Hindenburg's maiden flight on March 4, 1936, was a resounding success, demonstrating the capabilities of its design and engineering. Over the course of 1936, it completed 17 transatlantic crossings, proving its reliability and setting new standards for air travel.

Legacy of the Hindenburg's Design

The Hindenburg's construction represented the apex of rigid airship technology. Its design influenced later innovations in aviation, from materials science to aerodynamic principles. While its tragic end overshadowed its accomplishments, the Hindenburg remains a symbol of human ingenuity and the pursuit of progress, even in the face of formidable challenges.

In hindsight, the Hindenburg's design highlighted both the potential and the limitations of airship travel. It was a bold vision, executed with skill and precision, but ultimately constrained by the technological and political realities of its time.

As we delve deeper into the story of the Hindenburg, it becomes clear that its creation was not just about building an airship—it was about pushing the boundaries of what was possible, daring to dream of a future where the skies belonged to humanity.

Features and Specifications That Made the Hindenburg a Symbol of Luxury and Progress

The LZ 129 Hindenburg stood out not only for its monumental size and engineering but also for the luxurious experience it promised to its passengers. As a technological marvel and a status symbol of the 1930s, the Hindenburg epitomized progress in both aviation and passenger comfort.

Below, we explore the features and specifications that made the Hindenburg an icon of its time.

1. Grand Dimensions and Staggering Scale

The Hindenburg was the largest aircraft ever built, an awe-inspiring testament to human ambition:

- **Length**: 245 meters (804 feet), longer than three Boeing 747s placed end-to-end.

- **Diameter**: 41.2 meters (135 feet), making it one of the widest structures to take to the skies.

- **Volume**: The airship held a massive internal capacity of 200,000 cubic meters (7,062,000 cubic feet) of hydrogen gas, enabling its incredible lift.

The sheer size of the Hindenburg drew crowds of onlookers wherever it went, making it a symbol of human ingenuity and the technological progress of its time.

2. Luxurious Passenger Accommodations

The Hindenburg was designed to rival, and in some aspects surpass, the luxury ocean liners of the day. Passenger comfort was prioritized with the following features:

- **Main Deck (A Deck)**:

    o A **dining room** with elegant furnishings and seating for all passengers at once.

- A **lounge** equipped with a lightweight aluminum grand piano, allowing for live entertainment.

- A **writing room** offering a quiet space for passengers to write letters or read.

- A **promenade deck** with large panoramic windows, providing breathtaking views of the sky and earth below.

- **Cabins**:

  - Compact yet comfortable, the cabins featured a fold-down bed, a small table, and a washbasin. While lacking private bathrooms, they offered convenience and functionality within the constraints of airship travel.

  - Each cabin was lined with lightweight materials and soundproofing to enhance privacy.

- **Interior Decor**:

  - The airship's interiors were minimalist and modern, blending functionality with style. Lightweight aluminum and fire-resistant materials ensured safety while maintaining an upscale ambiance.

  - A mural in the lounge depicted the Graf Zeppelin's Arctic journey, adding a touch of artistic elegance.

3. Advanced Propulsion and Speed

The Hindenburg was powered by four Daimler-Benz DB 602 diesel engines, each capable of producing 1,200 horsepower. These engines provided:

- **Cruising Speed**: 125 km/h (78 mph), significantly faster than the fastest ocean liners of the time.

- **Range**: The airship could travel up to 8,000 kilometers (5,000 miles) without refueling, enabling transatlantic crossings in 2–3 days.

The efficiency and power of its propulsion system made the Hindenburg an attractive alternative for wealthy travelers seeking speed and comfort.

4. Cutting-Edge Engineering Innovations

The Hindenburg incorporated numerous advanced engineering features that set it apart:

- **Rigid Framework**:
  - Made of duralumin, a strong yet lightweight aluminum alloy, the framework formed a lattice of 15 main rings and longitudinal girders. This provided structural integrity while keeping weight to a minimum.

- **Gas Cells**:
  - The airship contained 16 hydrogen gas cells made from gelatinized cotton, allowing it to achieve lift while remaining stable.
  - The cells were designed to prevent rapid gas leakage and were equipped with pressure-relief valves to maintain balance.

- **Ballast System**:

    - The Hindenburg used water ballast to control altitude and stability. Water could be released or redistributed to adjust the airship's weight distribution during flight.

5. State-of-the-Art Navigation and Communication

Equipped with cutting-edge technology, the Hindenburg ensured safe and efficient navigation:

- **Radio Systems**: Allowed real-time communication with ground stations, a vital feature for long-distance travel.

- **Control Instruments**: Advanced altimeters, compasses, and barometers ensured precise navigation and altitude control.

- **Control Car**: Located below the airship's nose, this served as the operational hub, housing flight controls, navigation instruments, and communication equipment.

The airship's innovative systems represented the forefront of aviation technology in the 1930s.

6. Safety Measures

Despite its reliance on highly flammable hydrogen, the Zeppelin Company implemented several safety features:

- **Fireproof Bulkheads**: Divided the gas cells to limit the spread of potential fires.

- **Static Discharge Protection**: The outer fabric was treated to reduce static electricity buildup.

- **Emergency Exits and Equipment**: Ensured passenger and crew safety in the event of an emergency.

While these measures demonstrated thoughtful engineering, they were ultimately insufficient to counteract the risks posed by hydrogen.

7. Unparalleled Passenger Experience

The Hindenburg was more than just a mode of transport; it was an experience:

- Passengers enjoyed gourmet meals prepared by onboard chefs, accompanied by fine wines and spirits.

- Staff provided impeccable service, catering to the needs of every guest.

- The airship's smooth, quiet flight offered a serene and comfortable journey, free from the jarring turbulence often experienced on airplanes.

This level of luxury made the Hindenburg a preferred choice for wealthy travelers, diplomats, and celebrities.

8. A Symbol of National Pride

For Germany, the Hindenburg was more than an airship; it was a symbol of technological prowess and national pride. Its voyages were celebrated as feats of engineering and heralded as milestones in aviation history.

While its tragic end overshadowed its achievements, the Hindenburg remains a testament to an era when human ambition reached for the skies. The airship's luxurious features and cutting-edge specifications captured the imagination of millions and solidified its place in history as a marvel of progress.

CHAPTER 3

THE HINDENBURG'S MAIDEN VOYAGE AND SUCCESSES

The Hindenburg's inaugural flight and subsequent journeys marked a new era in air travel, showcasing the potential of airships as a luxurious and efficient means of transportation. This chapter explores the airship's first voyage, its rise to fame, and its operational successes, which captivated the world and solidified its place in aviation history.

The Maiden Voyage: A Bold Step Forward

The LZ 129 Hindenburg's first flight took place on **March 4, 1936**, a short yet crucial journey that demonstrated the airship's readiness to revolutionize long-distance travel.

Preparation and Launch

The anticipation surrounding the maiden voyage was palpable. The Zeppelin Company meticulously prepared for the event, ensuring every aspect of the airship's construction and operation was flawless.

- **Crew Training**: Extensive training was conducted to familiarize the crew with the Hindenburg's systems and operations.

- **Public Expectations**: As the largest aircraft ever built, the Hindenburg was under intense scrutiny from both the public and aviation experts.

- **Departure Point**: The airship lifted off from the Zeppelin base in Friedrichshafen, Germany, with a modest crew and no passengers aboard, as it was intended to be a test flight.

The flight was a resounding success, with the Hindenburg proving its stability, maneuverability, and reliability. The successful test paved the way for passenger flights and commercial operations.

First Passenger Voyage: A New Era Begins

The first commercial flight with passengers took place on **March 31, 1936**, marking the start of the Hindenburg's operational career. This flight transported dignitaries and members of the press from Friedrichshafen to Lake Constance and back, providing a preview of the luxurious airship experience.

Highlights of the First Voyage

- **Passenger Experience**: Guests marveled at the smoothness of the flight, the breathtaking views from the promenade windows, and the sumptuous amenities aboard the airship.

- **Performance**: The Hindenburg demonstrated its ability to cover significant distances at a steady cruising speed, laying the foundation for regular transatlantic flights.

The first passenger voyage generated significant media attention, with newspapers hailing the Hindenburg as a triumph of German engineering and a symbol of modern aviation.

Rise to Fame: Transatlantic Operations

The Hindenburg's fame grew as it began regular transatlantic flights, connecting Europe and the Americas with unprecedented speed and comfort.

Key Milestones

- **First Transatlantic Flight**: On **May 6, 1936**, the Hindenburg completed its first crossing of the Atlantic Ocean, traveling from Friedrichshafen to Lakehurst, New Jersey. The journey took just over 61 hours, a remarkable achievement for the time.

- **Passenger and Cargo Service**: The airship transported not only passengers but also mail and goods, establishing itself as a versatile mode of transport.

- **Cultural Impact**: The sight of the Hindenburg sailing through the skies became an emblem of modernity and progress. Crowds gathered at every landing site to catch a glimpse of the majestic airship.

Technical Excellence in Action

During its operational period, the Hindenburg proved its technical capabilities and reliability. The Zeppelin Company ensured that each flight adhered to strict safety protocols and maintenance schedules.

Operational Highlights

- **Efficiency**: The Hindenburg offered a faster alternative to ocean liners, reducing travel time across the Atlantic from weeks to just a few days.

- **Safety Record**: Until the tragic accident in 1937, the Hindenburg operated without significant incidents, cementing public trust in airship travel.

- **Prestige**: Wealthy individuals, celebrities, and political figures chose the Hindenburg for its comfort and status, further boosting its reputation.

Cultural and Political Significance

The Hindenburg's voyages were more than just transportation feats; they carried immense cultural and political weight.

- **National Pride**: For Germany, the Hindenburg represented a resurgence of technological prowess and national achievement during a period of economic recovery.

- **International Relations**: The airship's visits to foreign countries were often accompanied by diplomatic ceremonies and celebrations, enhancing Germany's global image.

- **Media Coverage**: The Hindenburg's flights were heavily documented by the press, with photographs and newsreels capturing its grandeur.

Passenger Testimonials and Public Enthusiasm

The passengers who traveled aboard the Hindenburg often described it as an experience unlike any other.

- **Comfort and Elegance**: Passengers praised the smoothness of the flight, the luxurious accommodations, and the attentive service provided by the crew.

- **Scenic Views**: The promenade deck offered unmatched views of the Earth below, from cityscapes to oceans, creating unforgettable memories for those aboard.

- **A Sense of Wonder**: Many passengers viewed their journey on the Hindenburg as a once-in-a-lifetime event, an experience that combined adventure with sophistication.

Public enthusiasm for the Hindenburg reached a fever pitch during its operational period, with ticket demand often exceeding availability.

Challenges Faced During Operations

While the Hindenburg's success was undeniable, it faced several challenges:

- **Hydrogen Concerns**: The use of hydrogen, though necessary due to helium restrictions, posed a significant safety risk.

- **Weather Dependence**: Airship travel was highly susceptible to weather conditions, which could cause delays or alter flight paths.

- **Economic Viability**: The cost of operating and maintaining the Hindenburg was high, making it a luxury service accessible only to the affluent.

The Pinnacle of Airship Travel

Despite these challenges, the Hindenburg's operational period was a testament to the potential of airship travel. It represented the peak of an era when humanity dared to dream big and reached for the skies with bold innovation.

The Hindenburg's success story was tragically short-lived, but its achievements remain a pivotal chapter in the history of aviation. Its journeys were not merely flights but milestones in the quest to conquer the skies, blending engineering brilliance with the spirit of adventure.

The Hindenburg's Role in Transatlantic Travel and Public Perception

The LZ 129 Hindenburg was more than just a marvel of engineering; it was a game-changer in the world of air travel, especially transatlantic crossings. It represented the future of travel during the 1930s, offering both speed and luxury on a scale that had never been seen before. Its journey across the Atlantic Ocean captured the imagination of the public and earned it a prominent place in the history of aviation. However, as much as the Hindenburg was celebrated, it also became a symbol of the era's technological ambitions and the dangers that accompanied them. This chapter explores the Hindenburg's role in transatlantic travel, its influence on public perception, and the cultural and technological impact it had on aviation and beyond.

Transatlantic Travel Before the Hindenburg

Prior to the arrival of the Hindenburg, transatlantic travel was dominated by ocean liners. The fastest and most luxurious ships, such as the RMS **Queen Mary** and the **Lusitania**, could make the journey from Europe to America in about four to five days, a remarkable feat at the time. However, air travel was beginning to make headway, albeit slowly. Airplanes were still relatively new, and commercial flight was not yet as reliable or comfortable as ocean liners.

For wealthy passengers, airships like the **Graf Zeppelin** offered a glimpse of what might be possible, but it was the Hindenburg that would truly capture the public's imagination and usher in the idea of air travel as the next big thing in transportation.

The Hindenburg's Introduction to Transatlantic Flight

The Hindenburg's first transatlantic flight took place in **May 1936**, when the airship crossed from **Friedrichshafen, Germany**, to **Lakehurst, New Jersey**, in the United States.

This flight was a turning point in airship travel. Although it had already completed several shorter journeys, this marked the beginning of regular transatlantic service.

- **Speed and Comfort**: The Hindenburg's ability to cross the Atlantic in **61 hours** was a significant improvement over ocean liners, which took longer. Its cruising speed of around 125 km/h (78 mph) made it one of the fastest methods of travel at the time, and it was far smoother than airplane travel.

- **Luxury Service**: Onboard, passengers were treated to a level of luxury unmatched by any other form of travel. The dining room served gourmet meals, and passengers could relax in a lounge complete with an onboard piano. The airship's amenities made it a floating palace in the sky.

- **Revolutionizing Transatlantic Flight**: While airplanes like the **Douglas DC-3** were beginning to provide commercial air travel across the Atlantic, the Hindenburg offered an entirely different experience. It combined the allure of air travel with the comfort of luxurious accommodations that ocean liners provided, positioning it as the next logical step in high-end transatlantic transportation.

The Hindenburg, thus, began to reshape the public's perception of what was possible in air travel, symbolizing the luxury and technological progress of the era.

The Role of the Hindenburg in Public Perception of Air Travel

The Hindenburg's fame was not solely based on its technical advancements or luxurious amenities. It was also an essential part of the public's growing fascination with aviation during the 1930s. This period was one of rapid technological innovation, with airplanes like the **Spirit of St. Louis** and the **Lockheed Electra** capturing the world's attention. The Hindenburg, in particular, became synonymous with the future of transportation.

Symbol of Technological Innovation

The Hindenburg represented the cutting edge of aviation. With its size, sleek design, and advanced systems, it embodied the aspirations of an era determined to conquer the skies. People were awestruck by its scale, fascinated by the engineering challenges involved in creating such a massive craft. It was not merely an airship; it was an icon of progress, representing human ingenuity and the potential to reshape the future of travel.

Cultural Icon

The Hindenburg's fame was amplified by media coverage. Newspapers, radio broadcasts, and newsreels extensively documented its voyages, and it became a symbol of national pride for Germany. Celebrities, politicians, and high-profile individuals often traveled aboard the Hindenburg, further elevating its status as the airship of the elite. It was an aspirational experience for many, something that few could afford but all dreamed of.

- The airship's sleek, modern design contrasted sharply with the older, more cumbersome ocean liners of the day, making it a striking visual representation of the future.

- The luxurious onboard experience and the visual grandeur of the Hindenburg made it an object of fascination, often depicted in popular culture as a mode of travel for the wealthy and powerful.

Public Reactions and Anticipation

Every time the Hindenburg arrived at a destination, it drew large crowds. In Europe and the United States, people gathered at airports and airship terminals to catch a glimpse of the massive craft. The Hindenburg was seen as a promise of a new world, one where travel would be faster, easier, and more comfortable.

The Hindenburg's Influence on Air Travel Perception

For the general public, the Hindenburg was the epitome of what air travel could be. Its size, luxury, and capabilities set it apart from airplanes of the time, and it helped shape the way people viewed aviation. While the Hindenburg was primarily a mode of transport for the wealthy elite, its success brought airship travel into the limelight and raised expectations for all future air travel.

- **Faster than Ocean Liners**: The Hindenburg's ability to cross the Atlantic in under three days made it a preferred option for those seeking to travel quickly, though its limited number of flights meant it was never a widespread option for mass travel.

- **Promoting Airships as Safe and Reliable**: Despite the inherent risks of hydrogen-based travel, the Hindenburg's seemingly flawless voyages built a strong reputation for airships as reliable forms of travel. Its ability to travel large distances with comfort and safety was a powerful message to the public about the future of air travel.

However, as with many technological innovations, the Hindenburg's legacy was marred by the ultimate tragedy that struck in 1937.

The Tragedy and Its Impact on Public Perception

The disaster that struck the Hindenburg on **May 6, 1937**, forever altered public perception of airships and air travel in general. The airship caught fire as it was attempting to land at Lakehurst, New Jersey, leading to the loss of 36 lives and the destruction of the airship.

The event was captured live on radio, and the shocking images of the Hindenburg bursting into flames were broadcast across the globe. The disaster marked the end of the golden era of airship travel and had a profound impact on public perception:

- **End of the Airship Era**: The disaster led to a swift decline in the use of airships for commercial travel, with airplanes emerging as the safer and more efficient option for long-distance flights.

- **Loss of Trust**: While the Hindenburg had been a symbol of progress, its fiery end cemented the dangers associated with airship travel, particularly the use of hydrogen as a lifting gas. Public confidence in airships plummeted.

Despite the tragedy, the Hindenburg's role in advancing transatlantic travel and shaping public perceptions of air travel remains undeniable. It helped push the boundaries of aviation and laid the groundwork for the future of flight, even as it tragically marked the end of an era.

Conclusion

The Hindenburg was a symbol of technological ambition, luxury, and the promise of a new age of air travel. It revolutionized transatlantic crossings and captured the imagination of the world, elevating airship travel to new heights of prestige. The airship's role in public perception was pivotal, as it embodied both the optimism and the perils of the early days of aviation. Though the Hindenburg's tragic end overshadowed its triumphs, it remains one of the most significant symbols of aviation history, representing both the aspirations of the past and the lessons learned for the future.

CHAPTER 4

THE FATEFUL FLIGHT – MAY 6, 1937

The Hindenburg's final voyage began like any other—calm, orderly, and full of promise. On **May 3, 1937**, the LZ 129 Hindenburg departed from its home base in **Frankfurt, Germany**, embarking on its 63rd flight, bound for **Lakehurst, New Jersey**. With 97 souls on board—36 passengers and 61 crew members—it carried not only people but also dreams of a world made smaller by the marvels of aviation.

This chapter recounts the journey from Frankfurt to Lakehurst, exploring the events leading up to the infamous disaster that forever changed the course of aviation history.

Preparations for the Voyage

The Hindenburg's transatlantic flights were a meticulously planned affair. In the spring of 1937, the airship was scheduled to make its first North American crossing of the season, marking the start of its regular service between Germany and the United States.

The crew, led by **Captain Max Pruss**, had prepared the airship to perfection. Maintenance checks were completed, weather conditions analyzed, and supplies loaded to ensure the comfort and safety of passengers. Among the cargo were letters and parcels, part of the airship's dual role as a passenger vessel and mail carrier.

The passengers were a mix of business professionals, tourists, and journalists, all drawn to the allure of the Hindenburg's luxury and speed. For many, this journey was an opportunity to experience the pinnacle of modern travel, an adventure they would recount for years to come.

The Departure from Frankfurt

On **May 3, 1937**, the Hindenburg lifted off from Frankfurt's airfield under clear skies. Spectators gathered to watch as the massive airship, over 800 feet long, gracefully rose into the sky. Its departure was a testament to the efficiency of the German Zeppelin Company, which had transformed airship travel into a symbol of national pride and technological superiority.

As the Hindenburg ascended, passengers settled into their cabins, explored the dining room, and took in the panoramic views from the promenade deck. Many kept diaries or sent letters describing the smoothness of the flight and the remarkable vistas of the European countryside below.

The Transatlantic Journey

The Hindenburg's crossing of the Atlantic was uneventful for much of the journey. Despite encountering occasional headwinds, the airship maintained its steady course, cruising at an altitude of about 650 feet. The experienced crew navigated the ship with precision, ensuring passenger comfort and safety throughout the flight.

Life Onboard the Hindenburg

Passengers enjoyed a level of luxury unparalleled in air travel at the time. Meals were served in an elegant dining room, featuring white tablecloths and fine china. The food was prepared fresh in an onboard kitchen, and the menu included gourmet European dishes.

The airship's lounge, complete with a grand piano, became a gathering place for passengers. They socialized, read books, and gazed out of the large windows at the ocean below. Some passengers remarked on the surreal experience of seeing both the stars above and their reflections on the water at night, a view only the Hindenburg could offer.

Approaching the United States

After nearly three days in the air, the Hindenburg approached the American coastline. Excitement grew among passengers as they prepared to disembark at Lakehurst, New Jersey. The crew worked diligently to ensure a smooth landing, as they had done many times before.

However, the airship encountered delays due to poor weather. Strong thunderstorms over New Jersey forced

Captain Pruss to delay the landing, circling the area while awaiting clearance. Passengers and crew alike remained patient, accustomed to the unpredictability of weather on transatlantic flights.

By the afternoon of **May 6, 1937**, the skies began to clear, and preparations for landing resumed. The Hindenburg descended toward the airfield at Lakehurst, its massive silhouette casting a shadow over the waiting crowd below.

Moments Before Disaster

As the Hindenburg approached its mooring mast at Lakehurst, the landing process was carried out with precision. Crew members released ballast to stabilize the airship, while ground crews prepared to secure the mooring lines. The atmosphere on board remained calm, with passengers gathering their belongings and anticipating a swift disembarkation.

At 7:25 PM, the Hindenburg hovered over the landing site, just 200 feet above the ground. Everything seemed routine— a testament to the efficiency of its experienced crew. The airship had completed countless landings without incident, and there was no reason to expect this one would be any different.

But within minutes, the unthinkable happened. As the mooring lines were dropped and ground crews worked to secure them, witnesses reported seeing a sudden flash of flame near the tail of the ship.

The Spark That Changed History

At approximately 7:30 PM, a fire erupted in the aft section of the Hindenburg. The flames quickly engulfed the hydrogen-filled airship, consuming it in less than 40 seconds. Passengers and crew scrambled for safety, some leaping from the burning wreckage while others waited for the airship to crash to the ground.

The once-pristine airship was reduced to a smoldering skeleton of twisted metal. Of the 97 people aboard, 36 lost their lives—13 passengers, 22 crew members, and one member of the ground crew.

Legacy of the Fateful Flight

The disaster was a defining moment in aviation history. The Hindenburg, once a symbol of human ingenuity and progress, became a cautionary tale of the dangers of early aviation technology. The fiery end of the Hindenburg marked the end of the airship era, as public confidence in hydrogen-powered airships evaporated overnight.

Despite the tragedy, the Hindenburg's final voyage remains a testament to the ambition and achievements of the Zeppelin Company. It also serves as a stark reminder of the risks that accompany great innovation. The legacy of the Hindenburg lives on, not only in the annals of aviation history but also in the lessons it offers about the pursuit of progress and the importance of safety in technological advancement.

This flight, though tragic, shaped the future of aviation by underscoring the need for safer, more reliable means of air travel—paving the way for the modern era of airplanes and jetliners.

Conditions Leading Up to the Disaster

The tragedy of the Hindenburg disaster was not an isolated event but rather the culmination of a series of conditions and decisions that set the stage for the catastrophe. To understand why the LZ 129 Hindenburg met its fiery end, it is essential to examine the factors leading up to that fateful day: the design and materials of the airship, the challenges of hydrogen as a lifting gas, operational decisions, and the immediate circumstances surrounding the landing at Lakehurst.

The Choice of Hydrogen Over Helium

One of the most critical decisions that shaped the Hindenburg's fate was the choice to use hydrogen as its lifting gas. Although helium was a safer, non-flammable alternative, it was largely unavailable to Germany due to geopolitical restrictions. At the time, the United States held a near-monopoly on helium production and refused to export the gas to Germany, fearing it might be used for military purposes.

The Zeppelin Company, therefore, had no choice but to rely on hydrogen, despite its well-known volatility. Hydrogen, though more dangerous, was lighter and more cost-effective than helium, making it the only feasible option for the Hindenburg's designers. This decision, while understandable given the circumstances, introduced a significant and unavoidable risk.

Flammable Coatings and Materials

The Hindenburg was a marvel of engineering, but its design included materials that contributed to the disaster. The outer skin of the airship was coated with a cellulose-based lacquer to protect it from the elements and improve its aerodynamics. Unfortunately, this coating was highly flammable and could ignite under the right conditions.

Inside, the hydrogen gas was contained within 16 large gas cells made of cotton and coated with a gelatin-based material to make them airtight. While effective for containing hydrogen, these materials were also susceptible to combustion.

Additionally, the airship's aluminum framework, though lightweight and strong, could not withstand the intense heat generated by a fire, contributing to the rapid structural collapse once the flames spread.

Weather Conditions

The weather on May 6, 1937, played a pivotal role in the events leading up to the disaster. The Hindenburg was scheduled to arrive in Lakehurst, New Jersey, earlier in the day, but strong thunderstorms in the area delayed the landing.

By the time the storms cleared in the early evening, the airship had been forced to circle the landing site for several hours, consuming valuable fuel and potentially causing additional stress on the airship's structure. The extended flight also increased the chances of static electricity buildup, a potential ignition source for the highly flammable hydrogen.

Witnesses later reported seeing lightning strikes in the vicinity of the airship as it approached the mooring mast, further underscoring the precarious weather conditions.

Static Electricity and Grounding Issues

The process of landing an airship like the Hindenburg involved dropping mooring lines to the ground crew, who would then secure the airship to the mast. This process required careful attention to the buildup of static electricity, which could accumulate on the airship's surface during flight.

In ideal conditions, the static charge would dissipate gradually as the airship descended. However, the prolonged flight and the humid weather may have caused an excessive buildup of static electricity on the Hindenburg's outer skin. When the mooring lines were dropped, the charge could have discharged in a spark, igniting the hydrogen.

Crew Fatigue and Human Error

Another contributing factor was the possibility of crew fatigue and human error. The Hindenburg's crew had been working tirelessly to maintain the airship's stability during the extended flight and prepare for landing under challenging conditions.

Some investigators later speculated that the pressure to adhere to the airship's schedule may have led to hasty decisions during the final moments of the landing process. Although the crew was highly trained and experienced, the combination of fatigue and the high-stress environment may have contributed to oversights that allowed the disaster to unfold.

Maintenance and Structural Integrity

In the months leading up to the Hindenburg's final flight, the airship underwent regular maintenance to ensure its airworthiness. However, some reports suggested that minor issues with its structure may have gone unnoticed or unresolved.

For example, there were rumors of small gas leaks in the hydrogen cells, which could have created an explosive mixture of hydrogen and oxygen within the airship. While these claims remain unverified, they highlight the inherent risks of operating such a complex and fragile machine.

Economic and Political Pressures

The Hindenburg was more than just an airship; it was a symbol of German technological prowess and national pride. The Zeppelin Company faced immense pressure to maintain the Hindenburg's impeccable record and promote airship travel as a viable alternative to ocean liners and airplanes.

This pressure may have influenced decisions to proceed with the flight despite unfavorable conditions. The desire to meet schedules and uphold the airship's reputation as a safe and luxurious mode of travel may have overshadowed concerns about potential risks.

The Last Moments

By the time the Hindenburg approached the mooring mast at Lakehurst, all these factors had converged to create a perfect storm. The airship's hydrogen-filled gas cells, flammable coating, and static electricity buildup were a volatile combination waiting for a spark.

When the spark finally occurred—whether from static electricity, a lightning strike, or another source—the result was catastrophic. Within seconds, the Hindenburg was engulfed in flames, and its once-majestic frame collapsed to the ground in a heap of smoldering wreckage.

A Lesson in Risk and Innovation

The conditions leading up to the Hindenburg disaster highlight the delicate balance between innovation and safety. The airship represented the pinnacle of engineering achievement at the time, but its reliance on hydrogen, combined with the inherent risks of its design and operation, made it vulnerable to disaster.

The tragedy serves as a sobering reminder of the importance of thorough risk assessment and safety precautions in the pursuit of progress. It also underscores the need for resilience and learning in the face of failure, as the lessons of the Hindenburg paved the way for safer, more reliable modes of air travel in the years that followed.

Key Figures On Board

The Hindenburg's final flight on May 6, 1937, was a microcosm of society at the time, with passengers and crew members representing diverse backgrounds, professions, and nationalities. Among the 97 people on board—36 passengers and 61 crew members—were prominent figures, individuals of note, and those whose stories have since become emblematic of the human side of this tragedy. Each played a role in the Hindenburg's legacy, either as survivors or as lives lost in the flames of history.

Dr. Hugo Eckener *(Honorary Mention)*

Although not aboard the Hindenburg on its fateful flight, Dr. Hugo Eckener played a pivotal role in the airship's history. As the former head of the Zeppelin Company and one of the most prominent advocates for airship travel, Eckener was a respected figure in aviation. His absence on the final flight has often been noted in historical discussions, as he was deeply involved in the development and promotion of the Hindenburg and its predecessors.

Dr. Eckener's cautious approach to airship safety and his opposition to Nazi propaganda use of the Hindenburg provide important context for understanding the political and operational backdrop of the disaster.

Captain Max Pruss

Max Pruss was the captain of the Hindenburg on its final flight. A seasoned airship commander with years of experience, Pruss was known for his meticulous attention to detail and commitment to his crew and passengers.

During the Hindenburg's landing, Pruss was in command, directing the complex procedures required to bring the massive airship safely to the ground. When the disaster struck, Pruss demonstrated remarkable bravery, staying aboard the burning airship longer than many others in an attempt to save lives. He suffered severe burns but survived the tragedy, later dedicating himself to recounting the events of that day to ensure the lessons of the disaster were not forgotten.

Chief Steward Heinrich Kubis

Heinrich Kubis holds a special place in aviation history as the world's first airline steward. His career began in luxury aviation, and by the time of the Hindenburg disaster, he was a veteran of airship service.

Kubis was instrumental in assisting passengers during the disaster. As flames engulfed the Hindenburg, he helped many passengers escape through windows and guided them to safety. His quick thinking and calm demeanor under pressure earned him recognition as one of the heroes of that tragic day.

Cabin Boy Werner Franz

At just 14 years old, Werner Franz was the youngest crew member aboard the Hindenburg, serving as a cabin boy. Despite his youth, Franz displayed extraordinary courage and composure during the disaster.

When the fire broke out, Franz was in the kitchen area of the airship. A burst of water from a ruptured tank doused him, allowing him to escape without serious injury. He quickly found a way out of the burning structure and survived the disaster unharmed. Franz's story became a symbol of resilience and bravery, and he later recounted his experiences to preserve the memory of the Hindenburg.

Passengers of Note

Margaret Mather

An American fashion designer, Margaret Mather was among the passengers aboard the Hindenburg. She was traveling to the United States to showcase her latest designs. Unfortunately, Mather was one of the 13 passengers who perished in the disaster. Her death was a loss to the fashion world and a poignant reminder of the human cost of the tragedy.

Adolf Hoepfner

A German businessman, Adolf Hoepfner was returning to the United States to oversee operations for his company. Hoepfner was known for his entrepreneurial spirit and connections between Germany and the U.S. Sadly, he did not survive the disaster, leaving behind a legacy of ambition and innovation cut short by the flames.

Leonhard Adelt and Gertrud Adelt

Leonhard Adelt, a German journalist and novelist, was traveling with his wife, Gertrud, aboard the Hindenburg. The couple was on their way to the United States for a literary tour and to explore new opportunities. Both survived the disaster, with Leonhard later providing detailed accounts of the events that unfolded, offering invaluable insights into the tragedy.

The Crew's Unsung Heroes

Helmsman Alfred Bernhard

As a helmsman, Alfred Bernhard was responsible for steering the massive airship. During the disaster, Bernhard remained at his post, trying to maintain control of the ship even as the flames consumed it. Though his efforts could not prevent the tragedy, his dedication exemplified the professionalism and bravery of the Hindenburg's crew.

Mechanics and Riggers

The Hindenburg's crew included a team of skilled mechanics and riggers who were responsible for maintaining the airship's complex systems and ensuring its structural integrity. Many of these individuals worked in the ship's lower sections, where the fire spread rapidly. Despite their efforts to contain the disaster, many perished in the flames, highlighting the inherent risks of their work.

Survivors and Their Legacies

Out of the 97 people aboard the Hindenburg, 62 survived, including 23 passengers and 39 crew members. Their stories offer a human perspective on the tragedy, shedding light on the resilience and courage displayed in the face of unimaginable horror.

Survivors like Werner Franz, Heinrich Kubis, and Leonhard Adelt dedicated much of their lives to sharing their experiences, ensuring that the lessons of the Hindenburg disaster were not forgotten. Their accounts provide a vivid and personal dimension to the historical narrative, preserving the memory of those who were lost and celebrating the bravery of those who endured.

A Snapshot of an Era

The key figures aboard the Hindenburg represent a cross-section of society in the 1930s—explorers, entrepreneurs, innovators, and workers. Their stories, whether of loss or survival, underscore the profound human impact of the disaster.

Through their lives, the Hindenburg becomes more than a symbol of technological ambition and tragedy; it becomes a deeply personal story of dreams, risks, and resilience, reminding us of the people who lived, worked, and died aboard one of history's most iconic airships.

CHAPTER 5

THE HINDENBURG DISASTER

A Step-by-Step Account of the Explosion and Crash

May 6, 1937, was a day etched in history not just for the tragedy but for the shocking and spectacular nature of the Hindenburg disaster. The event unfolded quickly, but every moment leading up to and during the explosion reveals a cascade of circumstances that led to one of the most infamous aviation disasters. This chapter provides a detailed, step-by-step account of the Hindenburg's explosion and crash, piecing together eyewitness testimonies, expert analyses, and photographic evidence to bring the fateful event to life.

Arrival at Lakehurst: A Routine Approach

The Hindenburg began its journey from Frankfurt, Germany, on May 3, 1937, and made a steady transatlantic voyage toward its destination: the Naval Air Station in Lakehurst, New Jersey. It carried 36 passengers and 61 crew members, many of whom had made similar trips before.

By the afternoon of May 6, the Hindenburg reached the skies over New Jersey. However, weather conditions delayed its landing. Captain Max Pruss decided to hold the airship in a circular pattern, awaiting clearance. By early evening, the weather improved, and the crew prepared to bring the ship down.

The Landing Procedure

At approximately 7:00 PM, the Hindenburg made its approach to the airfield. The landing was expected to be uneventful—a standard procedure involving the release of landing lines to ground crew members waiting below.

As the massive airship hovered over the mooring mast, ballast was released to stabilize the craft. The crew then deployed the landing lines, which were to be secured by ground personnel. At this point, all appeared normal, though some witnesses reported noticing a slight sagging at the rear of the airship, which they attributed to a redistribution of weight.

The First Signs of Trouble

At 7:25 PM, just as the Hindenburg was about to complete its landing, disaster struck. Observers on the ground and some passengers reported seeing a flash of light near the tail section of the airship. This was followed by a burst of flame that quickly engulfed the rear gas cells.

Hydrogen, the highly flammable gas used to lift the airship, began to ignite, causing a rapid chain reaction. Within seconds, flames spread along the entire length of the Hindenburg, transforming it from a majestic marvel of engineering into a fiery inferno.

The Explosion and Descent

The Hindenburg's framework, filled with 7 million cubic feet of hydrogen gas, became a tinderbox. The fire spread with such speed that those aboard had little time to react. Passengers and crew were thrown into chaos as the airship began to descend rapidly.

Eyewitnesses described the fire consuming the airship in under a minute, as the Hindenburg collapsed to the ground in a smoldering heap. Photographers and newsreel operators, present to document the landing, captured the disaster in real-time. These dramatic images and footage would later become iconic symbols of the tragedy.

The Human Response

Amid the chaos, acts of bravery and quick thinking emerged. Crew members like cabin boy Werner Franz and chief steward Heinrich Kubis worked to guide passengers to safety. Many passengers leaped from windows or openings in the airship's hull, risking injury to escape the flames.

On the ground, the landing crew rushed to assist survivors, pulling them from the wreckage and administering first aid.

Their courage and determination saved lives, even as the scale of the disaster became clear.

The Aftermath: Smoke and Ruin

By 7:30 PM, the Hindenburg lay on the ground, reduced to a skeletal framework of twisted metal. The once-proud airship was now a smoking ruin, its grandeur replaced by devastation. The disaster claimed the lives of 35 people aboard and one ground crew member, while 62 people miraculously survived.

The rescue efforts continued late into the night, with survivors transported to nearby hospitals. The site of the disaster became a scene of mourning and disbelief, as news of the tragedy spread rapidly around the world.

Eyewitness Accounts

The Hindenburg disaster was witnessed by dozens of people, including journalists, photographers, and members of the public. Their accounts provide vivid details of the event:

- **Herbert Morrison**, a radio journalist, recorded one of the most famous broadcasts in history. His emotional exclamation, "Oh, the humanity!" captured the horror of the moment and remains a poignant reminder of the tragedy.

- Passengers and crew described the fire's rapid spread, the heat of the flames, and the chaos as people tried to escape. Many recounted seeing others jump from the airship, some surviving the fall and others not.

A Tragic Chain of Events

The exact cause of the Hindenburg disaster remains debated to this day. While initial theories suggested sabotage, later investigations pointed to a combination of factors, including static electricity, flammable hydrogen, and the airship's outer coating.

Regardless of the cause, the disaster marked the end of the airship era. The risks associated with hydrogen as a lifting gas and the catastrophic failure of the Hindenburg shattered public confidence in this mode of transportation.

Legacy of the Hindenburg Disaster

The Hindenburg disaster is remembered as one of the most significant tragedies in aviation history. It serves as a stark reminder of the potential consequences of technological ambition, highlighting the importance of safety and innovation in equal measure.

The images of the burning airship and the stories of those who lived and died on that day continue to resonate, ensuring that the Hindenburg's story is never forgotten.

Eyewitness Testimonies and Radio Broadcasts

The Hindenburg disaster unfolded before the eyes of dozens of witnesses, many of whom were journalists, photographers, and members of the ground crew at the Naval Air Station in Lakehurst, New Jersey. Their firsthand accounts, coupled with one of the earliest recorded live radio broadcasts of a disaster, immortalized the tragedy in vivid and harrowing detail. These testimonies and recordings captured not only the technical details of the event but also the emotional weight of the disaster, offering an enduring glimpse into one of aviation history's most shocking moments.

Herbert Morrison's Iconic Radio Broadcast

Herbert Morrison, a reporter for Chicago radio station WLS, was present at Lakehurst to record the Hindenburg's arrival. His intention was to document the grandeur of the airship and the excitement of its passengers and crew. However, what unfolded turned his broadcast into one of the most famous recordings in history.

Morrison's narration began calmly, describing the Hindenburg's approach, its size, and the landing process. But as the disaster struck, his tone shifted dramatically, becoming frantic and emotional. His now-iconic words, "Oh, the humanity!" were uttered as he witnessed the airship engulfed in flames, passengers jumping for their lives, and the wreckage collapsing to the ground.

Key excerpts from Morrison's broadcast include:

- "It's burst into flames! Get this, Charlie, get this, Charlie! It's fire—and it's crashing! Oh my, this is terrible!"

- "Oh, the humanity, and all the passengers!"

The recording was not broadcast live but aired later, accompanied by newsreel footage, creating an indelible impression on the public. Morrison's raw emotion brought the tragedy into homes around the world, humanizing the disaster in a way no written report could.

Ground Crew Accounts

Members of the ground crew, who were preparing to secure the Hindenburg's landing lines, had a front-row seat to the disaster. Their testimonies provide crucial details about the moments before and during the explosion.

- **William Bishop**, a member of the mooring crew, recalled seeing a flash of light near the tail of the ship, followed by a burst of flames. "It was like watching a match being lit. It happened so fast, we didn't have time to react."

- **John Powles**, another ground crew member, described the intense heat and chaos as the burning airship collapsed. "People were running everywhere, screaming. We tried to pull survivors out, but the fire was overwhelming."

Passenger and Crew Testimonies

Survivors aboard the Hindenburg offered some of the most poignant and harrowing accounts of the disaster. Their stories reveal both the horror of the event and acts of extraordinary courage.

- **Werner Franz**, a 14-year-old cabin boy, was in the airship's kitchen when the fire started. He credited his survival to quick thinking and a burst water line that doused him with water, protecting him from the flames. He escaped through a hatch and jumped to safety.

- **Margaret Mather**, a passenger, described the moment the fire erupted: "I saw flames in the back, and then the whole thing seemed to go up at once. People were shouting and trying to get out. I don't know how I managed to jump."

- **Captain Max Pruss**, the airship's commander, stayed aboard until the very end, attempting to steer the ship and save lives. He suffered severe burns but survived, later describing the disaster as "an unimaginable nightmare."

Photographers and Journalists on the Scene

Several photographers and journalists were present at Lakehurst, eager to capture the Hindenburg's arrival. What they documented instead were some of the most iconic images of the 20th century.

- **Murray Becker**, an Associated Press photographer, captured a series of images showing the Hindenburg in flames, collapsing to the ground. These photographs were published worldwide and became synonymous with the disaster.

- **Sam Shere**, a photographer for the International News Photos, described the scene as "too fast to think. I just kept shooting as the flames swallowed the ship."

Reactions from the Crowd

Members of the public who had gathered to witness the Hindenburg's arrival provided their own recollections of the disaster. Many described the shock and helplessness they felt as they watched the airship burn.

- **Mary Johnston**, a local resident, said, "It was supposed to be a celebration. We came to see something amazing, and instead, we saw people die. I'll never forget the screams."

- **Franklin Harris**, a teenager at the time, recalled, "It was like nothing I'd ever seen before—huge, fiery, and terrifying. The whole field went quiet except for the fire and the cries of survivors."

The Emotional Impact

The collective testimonies and recordings convey not only the factual details of the disaster but also the profound emotional impact it had on witnesses and survivors. Herbert Morrison's tearful voice, the haunting images captured by photographers, and the stories of bravery and loss have ensured that the Hindenburg disaster remains deeply ingrained in public memory.

These firsthand accounts also provided investigators with vital information about the sequence of events, contributing to the understanding of what went wrong. The personal stories of survival and tragedy continue to resonate, reminding us of the human cost behind technological ambition.

Immediate Aftermath and the Chaotic Rescue Efforts

The Hindenburg disaster unfolded in a mere 34 seconds, transforming the proud symbol of engineering and luxury into a smoldering wreckage. While the fire consumed the airship with alarming speed, the immediate aftermath was marked by frantic and heroic rescue efforts as survivors, crew members, and ground personnel scrambled to save lives amidst the chaos.

The Wreckage and Initial Shock

As the Hindenburg collapsed to the ground, the scene at the Naval Air Station in Lakehurst, New Jersey, was one of sheer devastation. The once-majestic airship, 804 feet in length, lay reduced to a charred skeleton of twisted metal and burning fabric. Acrid smoke filled the air, and the cries of the injured and dying punctuated the chaos.

Eyewitnesses described the scene as apocalyptic:

- Ground crew member **Henry Schaefer** recalled, "It was impossible to believe that this enormous airship could be reduced to rubble so quickly. The heat was unbearable, and the fire lit up the sky like it was midday."

- Reporter **Herbert Morrison**, still shaken from his live commentary, noted the overwhelming sense of disbelief: "No one knew what to do at first. We were frozen, unable to process what had just happened."

Heroic Ground Crew and First Responders

Despite the inferno, members of the ground crew and nearby personnel sprang into action to rescue survivors. Many risked their lives, running into the wreckage to pull passengers and crew to safety.

- **William Buckley**, a firefighter stationed at the airfield, described the immediate response: "We had hoses ready for the landing, so we directed the water onto the flames. But it wasn't enough. The fire was too intense. We had to focus on saving people instead."

- Ground crew member **Frank Wilson** entered the burning wreckage multiple times to assist those trapped. He later recalled, "We didn't think about the danger. We just knew we had to help."

Rescuers formed makeshift human chains to carry survivors away from the blaze. Many worked with bare hands, tearing apart smoldering debris to free trapped individuals. Their actions were credited with saving lives despite the overwhelming odds.

Survivors' Struggles to Escape

For those aboard the Hindenburg, survival often came down to quick thinking and sheer luck. Passengers and crew members were forced to leap from the burning airship, many from heights of 20 to 40 feet, often landing in harsh terrain.

- **Werner Franz**, the cabin boy, recalled how he escaped through a galley hatch after a water line burst, dousing him with water and shielding him from flames. "I didn't think; I just ran and jumped," he said.

- Passenger **Joseph Spah**, a circus acrobat, used his agility to climb out of a window and leap to safety. He sustained minor injuries and was credited with saving a small dog on board by tossing it from the window.

Those who escaped the inferno often faced secondary injuries from burns, broken bones, and the chaotic stampede of rescuers and survivors fleeing the flames.

Medical Response and Triage

The Naval Air Station's infirmary and nearby hospitals were quickly overwhelmed by the influx of injured survivors. Emergency triage stations were set up on the airfield, where doctors, nurses, and volunteers worked tirelessly to treat burns, fractures, and other injuries.

- Dr. **Edward Burke**, a Navy physician, led the initial medical response. He recalled, "It was like a battlefield. The burns were severe, and many were in shock. We had to work quickly to stabilize them before transferring them to hospitals."
- Ambulances and private vehicles ferried the injured to nearby facilities, including the Paul Kimball Hospital in Lakewood and Jersey City Medical Center.

The medical staff faced immense challenges due to the severity of the injuries and the limited resources available. Despite these difficulties, their efforts were instrumental in saving lives.

Acts of Bravery Amidst Chaos

The disaster also saw extraordinary acts of courage and selflessness. Crew members like **Captain Max Pruss** and **Chief Steward Heinrich Kubis** remained on board as long as possible, helping passengers escape before making their own attempts to survive.

- **Captain Pruss**, who suffered severe burns while trying to steer the ship to safety, was praised for his dedication. Witnesses saw him shouting commands and assisting passengers even as flames engulfed the control car.

- **Chief Steward Kubis**, known for his calm demeanor, helped passengers locate exits and encouraged them to jump. His actions were credited with saving several lives.

Civilian Volunteers and Journalists

Civilians who had gathered to witness the Hindenburg's arrival also played a crucial role in the rescue efforts. Many ran toward the wreckage, ignoring the danger, to help pull survivors from the flames.

- **Mary Lancaster**, a local schoolteacher, recounted how she and others formed a line to pass water buckets to the firefighters. "We didn't have much, but we did what we could," she said.

- Photographer **Sam Shere**, who had captured the iconic images of the disaster, later joined the efforts to transport survivors to safety, saying, "Taking pictures felt trivial when there were lives to save."

Casualties and Survivors

Of the 97 people aboard the Hindenburg, 35 lost their lives, along with one member of the ground crew. The survivors, many of whom were severely injured, carried the physical and emotional scars of the disaster for the rest of their lives.

- Passengers and crew members who survived described the ordeal as a blur of heat, noise, and chaos.

- Rescuers later expressed profound grief over the lives they couldn't save, despite their heroic efforts.

The Aftermath

The wreckage smoldered for hours, attracting a somber crowd of witnesses, reporters, and investigators. The image of the charred remains of the Hindenburg became a stark reminder of the tragedy and the fragile line between human ambition and catastrophe.

The chaotic rescue efforts, though improvised and perilous, demonstrated the resilience and courage of those present. Their bravery in the face of unimaginable horror ensured that more than half of those aboard the Hindenburg survived, a remarkable feat given the scale and speed of the disaster.

CHAPTER 6

CAUSES OF THE HINDENBURG DISASTER

The Hindenburg disaster left the world in shock, prompting immediate investigations into the cause of the catastrophic fire. Experts, officials, and the public demanded answers to the pressing question: How could such a marvel of engineering and luxury be reduced to ashes in just moments? The investigations were thorough, but they left room for speculation and debate that continues to this day.

The Official Investigation

In the aftermath of the disaster, both the German government and the United States initiated inquiries to uncover the root cause. Led by the U.S. Department of Commerce and the

German Zeppelin Company, the investigations sought to determine whether the fire resulted from mechanical failure, sabotage, or a combination of factors.

Key findings from the investigation included:

- The fire originated near the upper tail fin (the stern) of the airship.

- Witnesses reported seeing a spark or flame just before the blaze erupted, suggesting an electrical discharge or static spark might have ignited the flammable hydrogen gas.

- The presence of highly flammable materials in the Hindenburg's construction, including its outer skin and gas cells, contributed to the rapid spread of the fire.

Static Electricity Hypothesis

One of the most widely accepted theories is that static electricity triggered the fire. As the Hindenburg approached its mooring mast at the Naval Air Station in Lakehurst, New Jersey, atmospheric conditions included high humidity and electrical storms earlier in the day.

- **Static discharge:** The airship's metallic framework and fabric covering may have accumulated a static charge during the flight. When the Hindenburg neared the mooring mast, the discharge could have sparked and ignited leaking hydrogen.

- **Leaking hydrogen gas:** The Hindenburg's hydrogen gas cells were vulnerable to small leaks due to wear and tear or punctures, potentially creating an explosive mixture of hydrogen and oxygen in the surrounding air.

Sabotage Theories

The dramatic nature of the disaster led some to believe it was the result of sabotage, especially given the political climate of the time. The Hindenburg's ties to Nazi Germany and its use as a propaganda tool made it a potential target for anti-Nazi resistance or foreign adversaries.

- **Suspicious claims:** A crew member, cabin boy Werner Franz, and others reported seeing strange activity near the stern of the airship in the hours before the disaster.

- **Political tensions:** In 1937, anti-German sentiment was rising globally, and the possibility of sabotage was considered by both German and American investigators.

However, no concrete evidence of sabotage was ever discovered, and the theory has largely been dismissed by modern historians.

Flammable Material in Construction

The Hindenburg's construction played a significant role in the disaster's severity. The outer skin was coated with a mixture of cellulose acetate and aluminum powder, materials that were later found to be highly flammable.

- **"Thermite" effect:** When exposed to heat or sparks, the combination of aluminum and iron oxide can create a chemical reaction similar to thermite, burning at extremely high temperatures.

- **Hydrogen fuel:** Hydrogen, while efficient and lightweight, is highly flammable. Its use as a lifting gas was necessitated by U.S. restrictions on exporting helium, a safer but more expensive alternative.

The combination of these materials created a "perfect storm" for a fire to spread rapidly once ignited.

Mechanical and Human Factors

Investigators also examined whether mechanical or human errors contributed to the disaster.

- **Stress on the airframe:** The airship's rigid structure experienced strain during the transatlantic journey, especially in turbulent weather. This could have caused damage to the gas cells, leading to leaks.

- **Landing procedures:** The Hindenburg's crew used landing ropes and ballast to stabilize the airship as it approached the mooring mast. These actions might have created static charges or allowed hydrogen to escape and ignite.

Modern Investigations and Analysis

Decades after the disaster, advancements in forensic science and engineering have allowed researchers to revisit the Hindenburg tragedy. Modern studies have largely supported the static electricity hypothesis, while some have pointed to additional contributing factors.

- **2000s reenactments:** In the early 2000s, researchers conducted experiments replicating the conditions of the Hindenburg's final flight. Their findings showed that a static discharge combined with leaking hydrogen could ignite the airship in a manner consistent with eyewitness accounts.

- **Alternative materials:** The flammable coating of the Hindenburg's skin was further scrutinized, with tests demonstrating how quickly it could ignite and spread flames.

A Tragic Lesson in Risk

The Hindenburg disaster revealed the inherent risks of hydrogen as a lifting gas and the dangers of using flammable materials in construction. The tragedy underscored the need for rigorous safety standards in aviation and engineering, leading to significant advancements in airship and aircraft design.

The disaster marked the end of the airship era, but it also served as a cautionary tale for future generations of engineers and designers. The lessons learned from the Hindenburg continue to shape the aerospace industry, ensuring that safety remains a paramount consideration in the pursuit of innovation.

The investigation into the Hindenburg disaster concluded that the combination of flammable materials, static electricity, and possibly human error created a catastrophic chain of events. While the exact cause may never be definitively proven, the disaster remains a powerful reminder of the delicate balance between ambition and safety in technological progress.

Theories: Hydrogen vs. Static Electricity, Sabotage, and Others

The Hindenburg disaster has captured public and scientific interest for decades, largely because the exact cause of the fire remains inconclusive. Several theories have been proposed over the years, ranging from the technical to the conspiratorial. This chapter explores the most prominent theories and the evidence supporting or refuting them.

The Hydrogen Theory

Hydrogen, the lifting gas used in the Hindenburg, is an inherently flammable substance. It requires minimal energy to ignite and burns with an almost invisible flame. Hydrogen's use in the Hindenburg was dictated by the geopolitical realities of the time: helium, a safer alternative, was tightly controlled by the United States, and Germany was unable to obtain sufficient supplies.

Evidence Supporting the Hydrogen Theory:

1. **Leaking Gas:**

   - The Hindenburg's 16 hydrogen cells were susceptible to leaks due to wear, manufacturing flaws, or damage sustained during the flight.

   - Witnesses reported seeing a gas-like vapor or hearing hissing sounds shortly before the fire began.

2. **Rapid Spread of the Fire:**

    o Hydrogen burns quickly and intensely, which would explain how the fire consumed the airship in just 34 seconds.

Criticism of the Hydrogen Theory:

While hydrogen played a role in fueling the fire, the theory does not fully explain the ignition source. Hydrogen leaks alone would not necessarily lead to combustion without a spark or flame to ignite the gas.

The Static Electricity Hypothesis

One of the most widely accepted theories is that static electricity caused the fire. This hypothesis suggests that a combination of atmospheric conditions and the airship's landing procedures generated a static discharge that ignited leaking hydrogen.

Evidence Supporting the Static Electricity Hypothesis:

1. **Atmospheric Conditions:**

    o The Hindenburg flew through thunderstorms earlier in its journey, potentially building up static electricity on its surface.

    o As the airship approached its mooring mast, the discharge of static electricity could have created a spark.

2. **Landing Procedures:**

    o The crew dropped landing ropes and ballast to stabilize the airship during its descent. These ropes touched the ground while the airship was still airborne, creating a potential path for static discharge.

3. **Eyewitness Reports:**

   o Several witnesses, including crew members and ground personnel, reported seeing a bright flash or spark near the stern, where the fire started.

Criticism of the Static Electricity Hypothesis:

While this theory explains the ignition source, it requires the presence of leaking hydrogen in the immediate area. The theory does not account for what caused the hydrogen to escape in the first place.

The Sabotage Theory

Given the Hindenburg's prominence as a symbol of Nazi Germany, the possibility of sabotage was a natural consideration in the investigations. Some speculated that the disaster was an intentional act designed to undermine the regime or target its propaganda efforts.

Evidence Supporting the Sabotage Theory:

1. **Political Tensions:**

   o By 1937, anti-German sentiment was growing worldwide, and the Hindenburg's use as a propaganda tool for Nazi Germany made it a high-profile target.

2. **Suspicious Activity:**

- Some witnesses claimed to see suspicious individuals or activities near the airship before its departure.

3. **Delayed Departure:**

   - The Hindenburg's departure from Frankfurt had been delayed, potentially giving saboteurs more time to plant an incendiary device.

4. **Internal Accounts:**

   - A crew member reportedly suggested the possibility of sabotage, though no conclusive evidence supported this claim.

Criticism of the Sabotage Theory:

- Extensive investigations by German and American authorities found no evidence of sabotage.

- The theory is often dismissed as speculative, fueled by the political climate of the time rather than hard evidence.

The Flammable Material Theory

Another significant factor in the disaster was the flammable materials used in the Hindenburg's construction, particularly the outer skin. This theory suggests that the materials themselves were a key contributor to the rapid spread of the fire.

Evidence Supporting the Flammable Material Theory:

1. **Outer Skin Coating:**

- The outer covering of the Hindenburg was coated with a mixture of cellulose acetate and powdered aluminum, a combination that is highly flammable.

- Tests conducted decades later revealed that the coating could ignite easily under certain conditions.

2. **Thermite Reaction:**

- The combination of aluminum and iron oxide in the coating could have created a thermite-like reaction, producing intense heat and accelerating the fire.

Criticism of the Flammable Material Theory:

- While the materials likely contributed to the fire's spread, they were not the initial ignition source.

- The theory does not explain the origin of the spark or flame that ignited the materials.

Other Theories

1. **Lightning Strike:**

- Some speculated that a lightning strike ignited the airship. However, no thunderstorms were reported in the immediate vicinity of the landing site at the time of the disaster.

2. **Fuel Leak:**

- Another possibility is that leaking fuel from the airship's engines or auxiliary systems created a flammable environment. However, this theory lacks strong evidence and was not supported by eyewitness accounts.

3. **Structural Fatigue:**

   - Some engineers suggested that stress on the Hindenburg's airframe during its journey might have caused a rupture in the gas cells, leading to the release of hydrogen. While plausible, this does not explain the ignition source.

A Complex Puzzle

The Hindenburg disaster remains one of the most thoroughly investigated tragedies in aviation history. Despite the wealth of evidence and analysis, no single theory fully explains the sequence of events that led to the fire. Most experts agree that the disaster resulted from a combination of factors: hydrogen leaks, static electricity, and flammable materials.

What is certain, however, is that the lessons learned from the Hindenburg have shaped the future of airship and aircraft design, ensuring that safety is prioritized in the pursuit of innovation. While the mystery of the Hindenburg may never be completely solved, its legacy endures as a reminder of the delicate balance between progress and caution.

Insights from Engineers and Experts

In the aftermath of the Hindenburg disaster, the investigation into its cause involved numerous engineers, aviation experts, and scientists. These experts brought different perspectives, shedding light on the many factors that may have contributed to the catastrophe. Their insights have helped refine safety protocols in both airship and modern aircraft designs, shaping the future of aviation. This chapter delves into the key insights provided by these professionals and what they believe may have been the cause of the fire.

Hydrogen and Its Risks

Many of the engineers involved in the investigation into the Hindenburg disaster pointed to hydrogen as the primary suspect. Despite being an efficient lifting gas, hydrogen is highly flammable and presents significant risks in confined spaces. Engineers highlighted that the airship's gas cells, which contained hydrogen, were vulnerable to leaks, especially given the Hindenburg's age and the wear on the material.

Expert Opinions on Hydrogen Use:

1. **Dr. Heinrich Linde, Airship Engineer:** Linde, a key figure in the design of the Hindenburg, argued that the use of hydrogen was inherently risky. While acknowledging the gas's effectiveness as a lifting agent, he emphasized that the ship's design should have focused more on minimizing the risk of leaks, given hydrogen's explosive potential.

2. **Edward T. Field, Aviation Safety Expert:** Field suggested that while hydrogen undoubtedly fueled the fire, the catastrophe was not simply the result of hydrogen leaks. The spark that ignited the gas was more likely to have been caused by some form of

electrical discharge, possibly static electricity or a short circuit in the ship's electrical systems.

Static Electricity and Discharge Mechanisms

The static electricity theory has long been one of the most debated in the wake of the disaster. Experts who focused on atmospheric and environmental factors suggested that static discharge could have ignited the hydrogen gas. Engineers analyzed the ship's approach to the mooring mast and the conditions during its final moments in the air.

Insights on Static Electricity:

1. **Dr. Hans Ritter, Atmospheric Scientist:** Ritter's research on atmospheric conditions indicated that the dry weather and high altitudes could have led to a buildup of static electricity on the airship's surface. He hypothesized that the high speed at which the ship was descending, combined with the movement of the gas cells, created the right conditions for a discharge to occur, especially as the ship neared the ground.

2. **Walter S. Jennings, Electrical Engineer:** Jennings focused on the interaction between the airship and the ground during the landing. He believed that as the Hindenburg was preparing to moor, the discharge of static electricity between the ship and the ground could have created the initial spark that set off the fire.

3. **General Conclusions on Static Discharge:** After decades of study, many experts believe that static electricity, while likely a contributing factor, was

probably not the sole cause of the explosion. Instead, it may have been the trigger that ignited the hydrogen once a leak had occurred.

The Role of Flammable Materials

The construction of the Hindenburg, while an engineering marvel, involved materials that contributed to the rapid spread of fire once it began. The outer skin of the airship was coated with a highly flammable material made of cellulose acetate and aluminum powder. This coating was designed to protect the ship from the elements but ended up playing a critical role in the intensity of the fire.

Expert Insight into the Role of Materials:

1. **Dr. Carl Schmitz, Materials Scientist:** Schmitz conducted extensive research into the materials used in the Hindenburg's construction. He noted that the combination of aluminum powder and cellulose acetate could combust easily when exposed to high heat. Schmitz theorized that once the hydrogen ignited, the highly flammable skin coating may have contributed to the fire spreading at a rapid pace.

2. **Walter Braun, Engineering Specialist:** Braun argued that the combination of the ship's lightness and the highly flammable coating contributed to the explosion's intensity. In his view, if the Hindenburg had been constructed with more fire-resistant materials or had incorporated design modifications to prevent the exposure of hydrogen gas to fire hazards, the disaster might have been avoided.

The Sabotage Theory: Expert Skepticism

While the sabotage theory was widely discussed at the time of the disaster, most experts remained skeptical. Engineers and investigators who scrutinized the wreckage of the Hindenburg found no clear evidence to suggest that the fire had been caused intentionally.

Engineers' Insights on Sabotage:

1. **Professor Ernst von Strauss, Engineering Expert:** Professor von Strauss, who worked with the German authorities investigating the disaster, argued that sabotage was unlikely. He pointed out that there was no indication of any incendiary devices or tampering with the ship's systems. His analysis concluded that the fire was likely accidental, possibly due to a spark near the gas cells.

2. **Maximilian Keller, Aircraft Safety Expert:** Keller also dismissed sabotage theories after analyzing the layout of the ship and conducting simulations of the disaster. He noted that given the complexity of the airship's systems and the absence of any forensic evidence pointing to a deliberate act, sabotage was highly improbable.

Conclusions on the Cause of the Fire

The cause of the Hindenburg disaster remains an open question for many, but experts and engineers involved in the investigation have generally converged on a few core conclusions.

1. **Multiple Factors at Play:** Most experts agree that the fire was caused by a

combination of factors, rather than a single point of failure. The highly flammable hydrogen, potential static discharge, and the vulnerable outer skin all worked together to create the conditions for an explosion.

2. **Design Flaws and Safety Oversight:** While the Hindenburg's design was innovative, it had some fatal flaws. The use of hydrogen, despite the known risks, and the ship's reliance on highly flammable materials contributed to the severity of the disaster. Experts believe that better safety measures, such as the use of fire-resistant materials and more rigorous monitoring of hydrogen gas cells, could have mitigated the risk.

3. **The Legacy of the Hindenburg Disaster:** As a result of the Hindenburg disaster, the use of hydrogen in airships was largely abandoned in favor of safer gases like helium. Additionally, new safety protocols in both airship and aircraft design were implemented to prevent such a catastrophic failure in the future. Engineers and experts agree that while the Hindenburg's fall was tragic, it was an important turning point in the evolution of aviation safety.

Final Thoughts

The Hindenburg disaster remains a fascinating case study in aviation history. The insights from engineers, experts, and investigators continue to shape the way modern airships and aircraft are designed, focusing on safety and risk management. Despite all the theories and analysis, the Hindenburg serves as a powerful reminder of the potential dangers inherent in technological progress, and the importance of learning from past mistakes to ensure the safety of future generations.

CHAPTER 7

THE HINDENBURG'S IMPACT ON AIR TRAVEL

How the Disaster Changed Public Opinion About Airships

The Hindenburg disaster marked a defining moment in the history of aviation. Its fiery demise on May 6, 1937, not only claimed 36 lives but also signaled the end of the airship era. Once seen as marvels of engineering and symbols of progress, airships quickly fell out of favor after the tragedy, reshaping public perception of aviation and its future. This chapter explores how the Hindenburg disaster transformed opinions about airships and spurred a shift toward the rise of fixed-wing aircraft in the public consciousness.

The Era of Optimism: Airships Before the Disaster

Before the Hindenburg disaster, airships symbolized innovation and modernity. They represented the potential for safe and luxurious travel across great distances. The German Zeppelin Company had established itself as a leader in this field, creating airships like the LZ 127 *Graf Zeppelin* and the LZ 129 *Hindenburg*, which were celebrated for their size, speed, and ability to cross oceans.

For years, airships were seen as a viable alternative to ocean liners, offering a faster and more elegant experience. The Hindenburg itself was a beacon of hope for this new mode of transportation, with its luxurious interiors and transatlantic capabilities. Its successful flights in 1936 reinforced the belief that airships were the future of long-distance travel.

However, this optimism masked the inherent risks of hydrogen-powered airships and their vulnerability to fire, a factor that would decisively alter public opinion after the Hindenburg disaster.

The Disaster and the Media's Role in Shaping Perception

The dramatic footage of the Hindenburg's fiery crash, accompanied by Herbert Morrison's emotional radio broadcast, had an unparalleled impact on the public. The disaster was one of the first aviation tragedies to be captured on film and widely disseminated through newsreels, photographs, and newspapers.

Herbert Morrison's Broadcast

Morrison's famous words—"Oh, the humanity!"—captured the horror of the scene and resonated deeply with listeners worldwide. His vivid account made the tragedy feel immediate and personal, amplifying the shock and fear associated with airship travel.

Photographs and Newsreels

Images of the massive airship engulfed in flames dominated headlines, cementing the disaster in the collective memory. The visual nature of the tragedy, combined with the scale of destruction, made it impossible for the public to ignore the dangers of hydrogen-powered airships.

The media coverage turned the Hindenburg from a symbol of progress into an icon of failure, altering public perception of airships almost overnight.

The Rise of Fear and Distrust

The Hindenburg disaster instilled a deep fear of airships among the public. Passengers who once marveled at the majesty of Zeppelins now viewed them as potential death traps. This fear was rooted not only in the dramatic visuals of the disaster but also in the realization that hydrogen, the primary lifting gas, was inherently dangerous.

Decline in Passenger Confidence

After the Hindenburg disaster, passenger demand for airship travel plummeted. Even the most loyal proponents of Zeppelin travel could not ignore the risks associated with hydrogen. Airlines and airship companies faced public scrutiny and declining interest, forcing them to reconsider the viability of this mode of transportation.

The Psychological Impact

For the public, the Hindenburg disaster became synonymous with aviation failure. People who had admired the elegance of airships now questioned their safety. The psychological association between airships and fiery destruction was too strong to overcome, leading to a steep decline in public trust.

The Shift to Fixed-Wing Aircraft

The fall of airships coincided with the rise of fixed-wing aircraft, which offered a safer and faster alternative for long-distance travel. The Hindenburg disaster accelerated this transition, as public and corporate focus shifted toward airplanes as the future of aviation.

Advantages of Fixed-Wing Aircraft

1. **Safety Improvements:** Airplanes relied on safer fuel sources and materials, reducing the risk of catastrophic fires.

2. **Speed:** Fixed-wing aircraft were faster than airships, cutting travel time significantly.

3. **Economic Viability:** Airplanes were more cost-effective to operate, making them appealing to both passengers and airlines.

Emergence of Commercial Airlines

By the late 1930s, commercial airlines like Pan Am and Lufthansa began expanding their services, offering transatlantic flights that competed directly with airships. The Hindenburg disaster gave airplanes a significant advantage, as passengers sought safer alternatives for international travel.

Impact on Aviation Safety Standards

The Hindenburg disaster also highlighted the need for stricter safety regulations in aviation. Although airships became obsolete shortly after the disaster, the lessons learned influenced the development of safety protocols for modern aircraft.

Hydrogen and Helium

The disaster underscored the dangers of hydrogen, leading to a global shift toward helium as a safer lifting gas. While helium was more expensive and less readily available, its non-flammable nature made it the preferred choice for airships in the years following the Hindenburg tragedy.

Materials and Design Innovations

Engineers began prioritizing fire-resistant materials and designs in both airships and airplanes. These advancements laid the foundation for the robust safety standards that define modern aviation.

The Legacy of the Hindenburg Disaster

The Hindenburg disaster remains one of the most significant events in aviation history. It marked the end of the airship era and the beginning of a new chapter in air travel, dominated by fixed-wing aircraft. While the tragedy was a devastating loss, it also served as a catalyst for progress, pushing engineers, governments, and the aviation industry to prioritize safety and innovation.

Today, the Hindenburg is remembered not only for its spectacular failure but also for its role in shaping the future of aviation. The disaster serves as a sobering reminder of the risks associated with technological advancement and the importance of learning from history to build a safer and more reliable future.

The Decline of Airship Travel and Rise of Airplanes

The Hindenburg disaster on May 6, 1937, was not just the end of a single airship; it marked the decline of an entire era of airship travel. Once seen as a promising and luxurious mode of transportation, airships were quickly overshadowed by the emergence of fixed-wing airplanes. This transformation was driven by the Hindenburg tragedy, advancements in airplane technology, and shifting public preferences for safer and faster travel.

The Golden Age of Airships and Its Rapid Fall

Airships were once the pinnacle of modern engineering. The German Zeppelin Company, with its innovations, established a reputation for luxury, reliability, and cutting-edge technology. Airships like the *Graf Zeppelin* and *Hindenburg* crossed oceans and continents, capturing the imagination of travelers and the admiration of the world.

However, the Hindenburg disaster exposed the vulnerabilities of airships, particularly their reliance on hydrogen, a highly flammable gas. The tragic images of the fiery crash burned into public consciousness, creating a fear that could not be undone. The event revealed that, despite their grandeur, airships were not the safest choice for modern travel.

Technological Limitations of Airships

Airships faced several inherent challenges that became more apparent after the Hindenburg disaster:

1. **Safety Concerns:** The use of hydrogen as a lifting gas posed a constant risk of fire. Even with safety protocols in place, the potential for catastrophe loomed over every flight.

2. **Weather Sensitivity:** Airships were heavily influenced by weather conditions. High winds, thunderstorms, and turbulence could severely disrupt flights, making them unpredictable.

3. **Speed and Efficiency:** While airships were faster than ships, they were significantly slower than airplanes. The leisurely pace of airship travel, once considered a luxury, began to seem impractical as air travel advanced.

4. **Limited Payload:** Airships had restricted capacity for passengers and cargo compared to airplanes, reducing their commercial viability over time.

The Rise of Airplanes: A New Era of Aviation

The decline of airships coincided with rapid advancements in airplane technology during the 1930s and 1940s. Fixed-wing aircraft offered solutions to many of the limitations faced by airships, propelling airplanes to the forefront of the aviation industry.

Speed and Efficiency

Airplanes were capable of traveling much faster than airships, drastically reducing the time required for long-distance travel. The ability to cross the Atlantic Ocean in hours rather than days appealed to passengers and cargo carriers alike, making airplanes the more practical option for modern transportation.

Safety Improvements

Unlike airships, airplanes used safer fuel sources and were constructed with fire-resistant materials. The adoption of stringent safety standards further enhanced their reliability, helping to rebuild public trust in aviation following the Hindenburg disaster.

Payload and Versatility

Airplanes could carry more passengers and cargo than airships, making them more cost-effective for airlines. Additionally, airplanes were less dependent on weather conditions, offering more consistent and reliable schedules.

Military Advancements

World War II played a significant role in advancing airplane technology. Governments invested heavily in aircraft development, leading to innovations that would later benefit commercial aviation. By the end of the war, airplanes had proven their versatility, reliability, and superiority over airships in both military and civilian contexts.

Shifting Public Perception

The Hindenburg disaster profoundly influenced public attitudes toward airship travel. Once associated with luxury and progress, airships became symbols of danger and outdated technology. The rise of airplanes offered a fresh start for aviation, with their speed and safety appealing to a new generation of travelers.

The Media's Role

The extensive media coverage of the Hindenburg disaster contrasted sharply with the growing success stories of airplanes. Newsreels, radio broadcasts, and photographs highlighted the dangers of airships while celebrating the achievements of commercial airlines.

Changing Aspirations

As society embraced a faster-paced lifestyle, the leisurely nature of airship travel became less desirable. Airplanes represented the future, offering a vision of progress that aligned with the modern world's demand for speed and efficiency.

The Legacy of Airships

While the Hindenburg disaster marked the decline of airship travel, it did not erase the contributions of airships to aviation history. Zeppelins played a crucial role in pioneering long-distance flight and introducing the concept of passenger aviation. The lessons learned from airship technology informed later developments in aircraft design and safety.

The Shift to Helium

In the wake of the Hindenburg disaster, the use of helium—a non-flammable lifting gas—became standard for the few airships that remained in operation. However, by then, airplanes had already become the preferred mode of transportation, relegating airships to niche applications such as advertising and sightseeing.

Cultural Impact

Airships remain an enduring symbol of a bygone era. They continue to capture the imagination through literature, film, and historical retrospectives, serving as reminders of both the promise and peril of technological innovation.

The Modern Era of Aviation

The Hindenburg disaster and the decline of airships paved the way for the modern aviation industry. Today's airplanes owe their success to the lessons learned from the airship era, particularly in terms of safety, engineering, and public trust. The disaster forced the aviation industry to confront its shortcomings and prioritize the development of safer, faster, and more efficient technologies.

As airships faded into history, airplanes took their place as the dominant force in global transportation. The transition marked the beginning of a new chapter in aviation, one defined by rapid progress and innovation. While the Hindenburg disaster remains a tragic reminder of the risks inherent in pioneering new technologies, it also serves as a testament to humanity's resilience and capacity for reinvention.

Lasting Changes in Aviation Safety Standards

The Hindenburg disaster of May 6, 1937, profoundly impacted the field of aviation, not only bringing the airship era to an abrupt end but also ushering in significant advancements in aviation safety standards. The tragedy underscored the importance of prioritizing safety in the development and operation of all aircraft. Lessons learned from the Hindenburg disaster reverberated through the aviation industry, prompting regulatory changes, engineering innovations, and a cultural shift toward stringent safety protocols.

Aviation Safety Before the Hindenburg

In the early days of aviation, safety standards were often rudimentary, with innovation and experimentation taking precedence over precaution. The rapid development of airships and airplanes was driven by competition and a desire to push technological boundaries. While some basic safety measures existed, they were far from comprehensive.

For airships, the reliance on hydrogen as a lifting gas was a known hazard. Although the German Zeppelin Company had a strong safety record prior to the Hindenburg disaster, the inherent risks of hydrogen's flammability were often downplayed or deemed manageable. The disaster highlighted the devastating consequences of such oversight and forced the aviation industry to reevaluate its priorities.

Post-Hindenburg Regulatory Changes

The Hindenburg disaster catalyzed the establishment of more rigorous safety standards for airships and airplanes. Governments, aviation authorities, and industry leaders recognized the need for greater oversight and accountability in aviation.

The End of Hydrogen in Airships

The most immediate change was the abandonment of hydrogen as a lifting gas. Airships that continued to operate after the Hindenburg disaster transitioned to helium, a non-flammable alternative. However, the scarcity and high cost of helium at the time limited the feasibility of large-scale airship operations, accelerating the shift toward airplanes.

International Collaboration on Safety

The disaster spurred international cooperation in developing safety protocols for aviation. Countries began to share information on best practices, leading to the establishment of standardized regulations governing aircraft construction, maintenance, and operation.

Strengthened Oversight

Aviation authorities such as the U.S. Civil Aeronautics Authority (later the Federal Aviation Administration) introduced stricter oversight of commercial aviation. Certification processes for aircraft and airship designs became more rigorous, requiring extensive testing to ensure safety.

Technological Advancements Inspired by the Hindenburg

The Hindenburg disaster highlighted critical vulnerabilities in aviation technology, prompting engineers to develop safer materials and systems.

Fire-Resistant Materials

The use of flammable materials in the Hindenburg's construction, such as its cotton fabric coated with a mixture of cellulose acetate and powdered aluminum, contributed to the rapid spread of the fire. In response, researchers focused on developing fire-resistant materials for aircraft and airship construction. These materials became standard in the aviation industry, significantly reducing the risk of onboard fires.

Improved Fuel Handling and Storage

The disaster underscored the dangers of improper handling and storage of flammable substances. Airplanes adopted improved fuel systems with enhanced containment measures to prevent leaks and minimize fire risks.

Enhanced Electrical Systems

The theory that static electricity may have ignited the Hindenburg's hydrogen highlighted the need for safer electrical systems. Engineers began designing more robust grounding systems and shielding for aircraft wiring to prevent sparks and other potential ignition sources.

Cultural Shift Toward Safety

The Hindenburg disaster profoundly changed how the aviation industry approached safety, fostering a culture of caution and accountability.

Public Demand for Safety

The graphic images and widespread media coverage of the Hindenburg disaster shocked the public and created a demand for safer air travel. Airlines and manufacturers recognized that safety was not just a regulatory requirement but also a critical factor in maintaining consumer trust.

Comprehensive Training for Crews

Aviation companies began investing in more comprehensive training programs for pilots, engineers, and crew members. Emphasis was placed on emergency preparedness, situational awareness, and adherence to safety protocols.

Safety as a Selling Point

In the competitive aviation market, safety became a key selling point for airlines and manufacturers. Advertising campaigns highlighted safety features to reassure passengers and differentiate companies from their competitors.

Legacy of the Hindenburg Disaster

The lasting changes in aviation safety standards resulting from the Hindenburg disaster extended beyond airships to influence the broader aviation industry. The lessons learned from the tragedy contributed to the development of the modern aviation system, which prioritizes safety at every level.

Catalyst for Modern Aviation Safety

The Hindenburg disaster served as a wake-up call, demonstrating the catastrophic consequences of inadequate safety measures. It set the stage for a more proactive approach to risk management, with aviation authorities anticipating potential hazards and implementing preventive measures.

Enduring Influence on Air Travel

Today's aviation industry operates under a framework of safety standards shaped by past tragedies like the Hindenburg. From the use of fire-resistant materials to the implementation of rigorous testing and certification processes, the legacy of the disaster is evident in every aspect of modern air travel.

A Safer Future

While the Hindenburg disaster marked the end of an era, it also paved the way for a safer and more reliable aviation industry. The changes it inspired have saved countless lives and continue to guide the evolution of air travel in the 21st century.

The Hindenburg disaster was a tragedy that transformed aviation forever. By forcing the industry to confront its shortcomings, it laid the foundation for the rigorous safety standards that underpin modern aviation. The lessons learned from the disaster serve as a powerful reminder of the importance of vigilance, innovation, and an unwavering commitment to safety in the pursuit of progress.

CHAPTER 8

THE LEGACY OF THE HINDENBURG

The Enduring Image of the Hindenburg in Popular Culture

The Hindenburg disaster transcended its immediate impact as a tragic aviation accident to become a lasting symbol in popular culture. Its dramatic demise has been etched into the collective consciousness, inspiring a myriad of representations in literature, film, art, and media. This chapter explores how the Hindenburg continues to captivate and influence various facets of popular culture, embodying themes of human ambition, technological vulnerability, and the fragility of progress.

Iconic Imagery and Symbolism

The Hindenburg disaster is one of the most photographed and filmed events of the early 20th century. The stark contrast between the airship's majestic presence and its sudden, fiery destruction has made its imagery a powerful symbol in various contexts.

Photographs and Newsreels

- **Murray Becker's Photographs:** Murray Becker, an Associated Press photographer, captured some of the most haunting images of the Hindenburg disaster. His photographs, showing the airship engulfed in flames and the chaotic rescue efforts, have become emblematic of the tragedy.

- **Herbert Morrison's Broadcast:** Morrison's tearful radio commentary, especially his famous exclamation, "Oh, the humanity!", paired with visual footage, immortalized the disaster in public memory. These recordings are frequently referenced in discussions about media coverage of tragedies.

Symbol of Technological Hubris

The Hindenburg has come to symbolize the perils of overreliance on technology and the unforeseen consequences of human ambition. It serves as a cautionary tale about pushing the boundaries of innovation without adequately addressing safety and ethical considerations.

Representation in Literature

The Hindenburg disaster has been a subject of fascination for writers, appearing in novels, historical accounts, and speculative fiction. Its enduring legacy in literature often explores themes of loss, technological failure, and the human condition.

Historical Accounts and Biographies

- **"The Hindenburg Disaster: The Last Flight of the LZ 129" by Michael Vogt:** This comprehensive account delves into the technical aspects, eyewitness testimonies, and the broader implications of the disaster, providing readers with an in-depth understanding of the event.

- **"Fire Over the Skies" by Ben Macintyre:** Macintyre's work examines the Hindenburg disaster within the context of Nazi propaganda and technological ambition, offering a nuanced perspective on its historical significance.

Fictional Portrayals

- **"Zeppelin Nights" by J.W. Guillory:** This novel reimagines the Hindenburg disaster within a fictional narrative, blending historical facts with speculative elements to explore alternate outcomes and the impact on individual lives.

- **"The Sky's the Limit" by Peter Pringle:** Pringle's science fiction story uses the Hindenburg as a backdrop for exploring themes of innovation, failure, and human resilience in the face of disaster.

Cinematic and Television Portrayals

The Hindenburg disaster has been depicted in numerous films and television programs, each offering a different interpretation of the event and its aftermath.

Documentaries and Historical Films

- **"Hindenburg: The Untold Story" (1994):** This documentary provides a detailed examination of the disaster, incorporating archival footage, expert interviews, and survivor testimonies to present a comprehensive narrative.

- **"The Hindenburg Explosion" (1940):** One of the earliest cinematic portrayals, this film dramatizes the disaster, blending factual events with fictionalized accounts to convey the emotional impact of the tragedy.

Dramatic Retellings

- **"Sahara" (1943):** While primarily a war film, "Sahara" includes a depiction of the Hindenburg disaster as part of its broader narrative, highlighting its role in the public consciousness during the era.

- **"The Lost Zeppelin" (1979):** This made-for-TV movie fictionalizes the Hindenburg disaster, focusing on the personal stories of passengers and crew as they navigate the unfolding catastrophe.

Artistic Interpretations

Artists have long been inspired by the Hindenburg disaster, using various mediums to capture its dramatic essence and explore its symbolic meanings.

Painting and Sculpture

- **"Hindenburg Burning" by Otto G. Frick (1937):** Frick's painting vividly captures the moment of the airship's explosion, emphasizing the chaos and destruction with bold colors and dynamic brushstrokes.

- **"The Hindenburg" by Eric Fischl (2008):** Fischl's sculpture interprets the disaster through abstract forms, evoking the sense of loss and the fragility of human creations.

Photography and Mixed Media

- **Ansel Adams' Photographs:** Though not directly photographing the disaster, Adams' work on airships and early aviation captures the grandeur and vulnerability of these majestic vessels, indirectly reflecting the Hindenburg's legacy.

- **"Smoke Signals" by Jenny Holzer (1989):** Holzer's mixed media installations use text and imagery to comment on the Hindenburg disaster's enduring impact on public memory and cultural narratives.

Music and Sound

The Hindenburg disaster has also influenced the world of music, inspiring compositions that evoke its dramatic and tragic nature.

Classical Compositions

- **"Hindenburg Symphony" by Samuel Barber:** This symphony uses orchestral movements to convey the rise and fall of the airship, blending somber melodies with intense crescendos to reflect the disaster's emotional weight.

Popular Music

- **"Hindenburg" by Iron Butterfly:** This rock song draws parallels between the airship disaster and personal turmoil, using the Hindenburg as a metaphor for explosive emotional breakdowns.

- **"The Hindenburg Disaster" by They Might Be Giants:** The band's song incorporates historical references and a catchy tune to educate listeners about the disaster while keeping it engaging and memorable.

The Hindenburg in Modern Media and Technology

In addition to traditional forms of media, the Hindenburg disaster continues to influence modern technology and digital representations.

Video Games and Virtual Reality

- **"Assassin's Creed: Syndicate" (2015):** This popular video game includes a fictionalized version of the Hindenburg disaster, allowing players to interact with the event through immersive gameplay.

- **Virtual Reality Simulations:** VR experiences recreate the Hindenburg disaster, offering users a first-person perspective of the tragedy and its immediate aftermath, enhancing historical empathy and understanding.

Online Memes and Pop Culture References

- **"Oh, the humanity!" Meme:** Herbert Morrison's famous phrase has been repurposed in internet culture as a meme, often used humorously to exaggerate minor inconveniences or dramatic reactions.

- **Documentary Series and YouTube Channels:** Numerous online platforms feature detailed analyses and re-enactments of the Hindenburg disaster, making its legacy accessible to new generations through digital storytelling.

Educational Impact and Historical Significance

The Hindenburg disaster remains a pivotal case study in aviation history, safety engineering, and media studies, influencing educational curricula and research.

Aviation Safety Training

- **Case Studies:** The disaster is frequently used as a case study in aviation safety courses, highlighting the importance of risk management, material science, and emergency preparedness.

- **Engineering Education:** Engineering programs incorporate lessons from the Hindenburg disaster to teach about the complexities of large-scale project management, structural integrity, and the unintended consequences of material choices.

Media Studies

- **Journalism Courses:** Morrison's broadcast is analyzed in journalism courses to understand the role of media in shaping public perception and documenting historical events.

- **Film and Media Analysis:** The Hindenburg's portrayal in various media forms is studied to explore how disasters are represented and remembered in popular culture.

The Survivors and Their Lives After the Crash

The Hindenburg disaster on May 6, 1937, claimed the lives of 36 people, but remarkably, 62 of the 97 individuals aboard survived. For those who lived through the inferno, survival marked the beginning of a new chapter—a life overshadowed by the harrowing memories of the fiery crash. These survivors came from diverse backgrounds: passengers traveling in luxury, crew members dedicated to the airship, and journalists covering its transatlantic journey. This chapter delves into the lives of these individuals after the disaster, exploring how they coped with the physical, emotional, and psychological scars they carried.

The Survivors' Stories

Passengers

Among the passengers were prominent figures and ordinary travelers, each with a unique reason for being aboard the Hindenburg. Their survival stories often depended on sheer luck, quick thinking, and the heroic actions of others.

- **Margaret Mather: The Actress Who Escaped the Flames**
  Margaret Mather, a well-known actress traveling aboard the Hindenburg, managed to leap from a window just as the airship descended. Though she sustained injuries, her fame brought attention to the survivors' experiences. Mather became an advocate for aviation safety, using her platform to discuss the need for stricter regulations in air travel.

- **Gerard F. Adams: A Businessman's Harrowing Escape**
  Adams, an American businessman, recalled his miraculous escape through a broken observation window. Despite suffering from burns, he credited the swift actions of the ground crew for saving his life. After the disaster, Adams avoided air travel entirely, choosing to focus on expanding his business ventures.

Crew Members

The Hindenburg's crew, familiar with the airship's layout and operations, often acted as first responders during the disaster. Many of them displayed extraordinary bravery, assisting passengers even as their own lives were at risk.

- **Werner Franz: The Teenaged Cabin Boy**
  Werner Franz, just 14 years old at the time, was the youngest crew member aboard the Hindenburg. As the airship caught fire, Franz managed to escape after a burst water tank doused the flames around him, giving him a chance to reach safety. He went on to live a long life, often speaking publicly about his experience and the camaraderie of the crew.

- **Heinrich Kubis: The Steward Who Saved Lives** Heinrich Kubis, the chief steward, played a pivotal role in helping passengers escape through the dining room windows. His calm demeanor and quick thinking saved numerous lives. Kubis continued working in aviation, becoming an advocate for safety improvements in airship design.

Journalists and Observers

Several journalists were aboard the Hindenburg to document its historic transatlantic journey. Their experiences became an essential part of the narrative surrounding the disaster.

- **Leonhard Adelt: The Writer-Turned-Survivor** Leonhard Adelt, a German journalist, survived alongside his wife, Gertrud. Adelt's firsthand account of the disaster became one of the earliest and most detailed reports, capturing the chaos and heroism of that fateful day. His writings helped preserve the human side of the tragedy, highlighting the resilience and bravery of those aboard.

Life After the Disaster

For many survivors, the Hindenburg disaster marked a turning point in their lives. The physical injuries—burns, broken bones, and scars—were often accompanied by deep emotional trauma.

Physical Recovery and Challenges

Survivors who sustained injuries required extensive medical care. Burn treatments in the 1930s were primitive compared to modern standards, making recovery a painful and prolonged process. Many survivors bore visible scars, which served as constant reminders of the disaster.

- **Innovations in Burn Treatment**
  The Hindenburg disaster indirectly contributed to advancements in burn care, as doctors experimented with new techniques to treat the injured. Survivors like Margaret Mather participated in early skin graft trials, paving the way for future medical breakthroughs.

Emotional and Psychological Impact

The trauma of surviving such a catastrophic event left deep psychological scars. Survivors often grappled with survivor's guilt, flashbacks, and anxiety.

- **Coping Mechanisms**
  Some survivors sought solace in advocacy, using their experiences to push for improvements in aviation safety. Others retreated from public life, struggling to reconcile their survival with the loss of friends, colleagues, and loved ones.

- **Resilience and Heroism**
  Despite their struggles, many survivors displayed remarkable resilience. They formed lifelong bonds with fellow survivors, finding strength in shared experiences. Their stories of bravery and survival inspired countless others, becoming symbols of hope and perseverance.

Public Recognition and Commemoration

The survivors of the Hindenburg disaster became living reminders of the event. Over the years, their stories were celebrated, documented, and honored in various ways.

- **Reunions and Memorials** Annual reunions of survivors and their families became opportunities to commemorate those lost and celebrate the resilience of those who survived. The Naval Air Station Lakehurst, where the Hindenburg crashed, became a site for memorial services and historical exhibitions.

- **Interviews and Documentaries** Survivors like Werner Franz and Margaret Mather shared their stories in interviews and documentaries, ensuring that the human side of the disaster was never forgotten. Their firsthand accounts provided valuable insights into the events of that day, enriching the historical narrative.

A Lasting Legacy

The lives of the Hindenburg survivors offer powerful lessons in courage, resilience, and the human capacity to endure. Their experiences underscore the importance of safety in aviation and the need to remember history's tragedies to prevent future ones.

As time passed, the number of living survivors dwindled, but their stories continued to inspire. Through books, films, and commemorations, the legacy of the Hindenburg disaster—and the lives it touched—remains a vital part of aviation history.

Memorials and Honors for Those Who Perished

The Hindenburg disaster was one of the most tragic and visually impactful events of the 20th century. The loss of 36 lives, including passengers, crew members, and one worker on the ground, shocked the world and left a lasting impression on the history of aviation. Memorials and honors dedicated to those who perished serve as solemn reminders of the tragedy, ensuring their stories are not forgotten. Over the decades, various commemorations have taken place to honor the victims, celebrate the bravery of the survivors, and educate future generations about the event.

Immediate Responses: Mourning the Losses

In the immediate aftermath of the disaster, mourning ceremonies were held both in Germany and the United States. These gatherings reflected the shared grief of two nations and underscored the global impact of the tragedy.

Funeral Services

- **In Germany**: The German Zeppelin Company organized a solemn service in Friedrichshafen, the Hindenburg's home base, to honor the crew and passengers who had perished. This event was attended by grieving families, company officials, and aviation enthusiasts. Wreaths and flowers were placed near Zeppelin monuments as symbols of respect.

- **In the United States**: Funeral services for American victims were held across the country. In New York City, a public memorial service drew hundreds of mourners, emphasizing the transatlantic connection of the Hindenburg's passengers.

National Flags at Half-Mast

Both Germany and the United States flew their national flags at half-mast to honor the victims, reflecting the shared sense of loss between the two nations.

The Lakehurst Naval Air Station Memorial

The site of the Hindenburg crash, the Lakehurst Naval Air Station in New Jersey, has become the most significant location for honoring the victims.

The Hindenburg Crash Marker

In 1938, a simple concrete marker was placed at the exact spot where the airship's gondola came to rest. The marker bears the inscription: *"Site of the Hindenburg Disaster, May 6, 1937."*

Annual Memorial Services

Every year on May 6, a memorial service is held at the crash site to commemorate the anniversary of the disaster. These ceremonies are attended by aviation historians, local residents, and occasionally, descendants of the victims and survivors.

Educational Outreach

The crash site at Lakehurst is preserved as a historical landmark. Guided tours led by military personnel and historians provide visitors with insights into the disaster. A small museum nearby houses artifacts, photographs, and documents related to the Hindenburg, serving as a tribute to those who perished.

Honoring the Crew

Special recognition has been given to the crew members who died in the line of duty. These individuals were remembered for their professionalism and bravery during the disaster.

German Zeppelin Company Tributes

The German Zeppelin Company established a memorial in Friedrichshafen to honor the crew of the Hindenburg. This tribute includes a plaque listing the names of the deceased crew members and recognizes their contributions to advancing airship travel.

Commemorative Medals

In Germany, commemorative medals were issued in memory of the Hindenburg crew. These medals depicted the airship alongside the Zeppelin logo and served as keepsakes for families of the victims.

Public Memorials in Germany and the United States

Over the years, various public memorials have been established to honor those who perished in the Hindenburg disaster.

Friedrichshafen Zeppelin Museum

The Zeppelin Museum in Friedrichshafen, Germany, features a dedicated section for the Hindenburg disaster. This exhibit includes personal belongings of the victims, photographs, and a detailed timeline of the event. A wall of remembrance displays the names of all who died, serving as a poignant tribute.

American Aviation Museums

Several aviation museums across the United States, including the Smithsonian National Air and Space Museum, have dedicated exhibits to the Hindenburg. These displays highlight the disaster's historical significance and commemorate the lives lost.

Commemorative Publications and Documentaries

Over the years, numerous books, documentaries, and articles have been published to keep the memory of the Hindenburg disaster alive. These works often include dedications to the victims, ensuring their stories are shared with future generations.

Prominent Works

- **Herbert Morrison's Iconic Broadcast**: Morrison's haunting radio commentary during the disaster immortalized the phrase, *"Oh, the humanity!"* His broadcast served as an unintentional tribute to the lives lost, capturing the raw emotion of the tragedy.

- **Documentary Films**: Documentaries such as *Hindenburg: The Untold Story* include poignant tributes to the victims, often featuring interviews with survivors and family members.

Artistic Tributes

The Hindenburg disaster has inspired numerous artistic works that honor the memory of those who perished. Paintings, sculptures, and literary works often portray the tragic beauty of the event while paying homage to its victims.

Memorial Paintings

Artists have created striking visual interpretations of the disaster, focusing on the human aspect of the tragedy. These works are displayed in museums and galleries worldwide.

Literary Memorials

Poems and novels inspired by the Hindenburg disaster often include dedications to the victims. These literary pieces serve as a form of remembrance, preserving the emotional impact of the event.

Modern-Day Recognition

As the years have passed, the Hindenburg disaster continues to hold a significant place in collective memory. Efforts to honor the victims have expanded, incorporating new technologies and platforms.

Digital Memorials

Online memorials and virtual tours of the Lakehurst crash site provide a global audience with the opportunity to learn about the disaster and pay their respects. Websites dedicated to aviation history often feature pages commemorating the Hindenburg's victims.

Social Media Tributes

On anniversaries of the disaster, aviation enthusiasts and historians share tributes on social media platforms. These posts often include photographs, survivor accounts, and reflections on the event's legacy.

Conclusion

The memorials and honors dedicated to those who perished in the Hindenburg disaster serve as enduring reminders of the lives lost on that fateful day. Through physical monuments, museum exhibits, artistic works, and digital platforms, their stories continue to resonate. These tributes not only honor the victims but also remind us of the importance of safety and innovation in the pursuit of progress.

CHAPTER 9

REASSESSING THE DISASTER – MYTHS VS. FACTS

The Hindenburg disaster has become one of the most iconic events in aviation history, but the tragedy has also been shrouded in myths, misconceptions, and sensationalized theories. These narratives often obscure the truth and perpetuate misunderstandings about what truly happened on May 6, 1937. This chapter aims to debunk some of the most common myths surrounding the Hindenburg disaster by separating fact from fiction, relying on historical records, eyewitness accounts, and modern scientific analysis.

Myth 1: The Hindenburg Was Sabotaged

One of the most persistent theories about the Hindenburg disaster is that it was caused by sabotage. Some have speculated that an explosive device or incendiary act led to the catastrophic fire.

Origins of the Myth

- In the tense political climate of the 1930s, the Hindenburg's association with Nazi Germany fueled suspicions that the disaster was a targeted attack.

- Early on, the German Zeppelin Company and officials in Nazi Germany sought to distance themselves from technical failures, which led to the promotion of sabotage as a possible cause.

Debunking the Myth

- **Lack of Evidence**: Despite thorough investigations by both American and German authorities, no credible evidence of sabotage was ever found. No explosive residues, suspicious individuals, or other indicators supported this theory.

- **Expert Opinions**: Modern scientists and historians have reviewed the evidence and consistently ruled out sabotage as a likely cause, citing technical issues as the more plausible explanation.

Myth 2: The Hindenburg Was Filled with Hydrogen Instead of Helium Due to Nazi Ideology

A common misconception is that the Hindenburg's use of hydrogen instead of helium was a deliberate choice by the Nazis, either to cut costs or as a show of technological defiance.

Origins of the Myth

- The political climate of the time led to assumptions that Nazi Germany preferred hydrogen to demonstrate self-reliance and disregard for safer alternatives.

- Some speculated that helium, a non-flammable gas, was rejected out of sheer arrogance or ideological stubbornness.

Debunking the Myth

- **Helium Embargo**: The true reason for using hydrogen was the U.S. embargo on helium exports to Germany. Helium was a rare and valuable resource, and the United States controlled the world's largest reserves. The political tensions of the 1930s prevented Germany from obtaining the helium needed for the Hindenburg.

- **Technological Considerations**: Hydrogen, although flammable, was lighter and provided greater lift than helium, making it a practical (though risky) choice for large airships like the Hindenburg.

Myth 3: The Paint on the Hindenburg Was Highly Flammable

Another popular theory suggests that the Hindenburg's outer fabric was coated with a highly flammable paint, which contributed to the rapid spread of the fire.

Origins of the Myth

- Some proponents of this theory likened the outer skin's materials to substances used in rocket fuel, suggesting the disaster was almost inevitable.

- This claim gained traction in the late 20th century after independent researchers conducted experiments on similar materials.

Debunking the Myth

- **Scientific Analysis**: While the Hindenburg's fabric contained aluminum and iron oxide, modern tests have shown that these materials were not as volatile as initially claimed. The rapid spread of the fire was more likely caused by the hydrogen gas escaping from the ruptured cells rather than the fabric itself.

- **Primary Cause**: The prevailing consensus is that the hydrogen ignited first, and the fabric burned as a secondary effect rather than as the primary fuel source.

Myth 4: Lightning Directly Struck the Hindenburg

A popular theory suggests that the disaster was caused by a lightning strike, which ignited the hydrogen within the airship.

Origins of the Myth

- Stormy weather in the Lakehurst area on the day of the disaster led to speculation that lightning might have been responsible.

- Eyewitness accounts describing flashes of light before the fire further fueled this belief.

Debunking the Myth

- **Weather Conditions**: While there were storms earlier in the day, the weather had largely cleared by the time the Hindenburg attempted to land. No evidence of a direct lightning strike was found during investigations.

- **Static Electricity**: Investigators and modern researchers suggest that static electricity, rather than lightning, was more likely the culprit. The buildup of static charges combined with leaking hydrogen created the perfect conditions for ignition.

Myth 5: Everyone on Board Died in the Disaster

The fiery destruction of the Hindenburg was so dramatic that many assume all passengers and crew perished in the disaster.

Origins of the Myth

- The intensity of the fire, captured in photographs and Herbert Morrison's famous radio broadcast, led to the impression that survival was impossible.

- Early media reports focused heavily on the fatalities, often overshadowing stories of survival.

Debunking the Myth

- **Survival Rates**: Out of the 97 people on board, 62 survived the disaster. Many were able to jump to safety or were rescued from the wreckage.

- **Heroic Efforts**: The actions of the ground crew and surviving crew members played a significant role in the high survival rate, particularly given the speed of the fire's spread.

Myth 6: The Hindenburg Was Doomed from the Start

Some myths suggest that the Hindenburg was inherently flawed and that its destruction was inevitable.

Origins of the Myth

- The dramatic nature of the disaster has led to hindsight bias, with people viewing the Hindenburg as a doomed vessel from its inception.

- Critics of airship travel often retroactively labeled the technology as inherently dangerous.

Debunking the Myth

- **Track Record**: The Hindenburg had completed numerous successful flights before the disaster, including transatlantic crossings. It was considered a reliable and groundbreaking achievement in airship engineering.

- **Historical Context**: While hydrogen-filled airships posed risks, they were not viewed as catastrophically flawed for their time. The Hindenburg disaster was a turning point, not an inevitability.

Modern Perspectives on the Tragedy

The Hindenburg disaster continues to captivate historians, engineers, and the public, serving as a symbol of both human ingenuity and the catastrophic consequences of technological failure. In the years since the airship's fiery demise on May 6, 1937, our understanding of the tragedy has evolved. Advances in engineering, scientific analysis, and historical research have provided fresh insights into the disaster, reshaping how we view it in the context of both its time and ours.

The Hindenburg as a Case Study in Risk and Innovation

Modern historians and engineers often examine the Hindenburg disaster as a pivotal moment in the history of innovation, highlighting the balance between risk-taking and safety in technological advancement.

Innovation's High Stakes

- The Hindenburg represented the pinnacle of airship technology in the 1930s. It was a marvel of engineering, luxury, and ambition, pushing the boundaries of what was possible in transatlantic travel.

- However, the reliance on hydrogen—a highly flammable gas—illustrates the inherent risks in technological progress. Modern safety protocols in aviation and other industries emphasize the importance of mitigating such risks through redundancy, material science, and rigorous testing.

Lessons Learned

- The Hindenburg disaster underscores the need for adaptability and openness to new solutions. The reluctance or inability to use safer alternatives, such as helium, proved to be a fatal flaw.

- Today's engineers often cite the Hindenburg as an example of why safety must be prioritized, even when innovation and economic pressures tempt shortcuts.

Scientific and Technological Insights

Advances in materials science, forensics, and aerodynamics have allowed modern experts to revisit the technical aspects of the disaster.

Reevaluating the Cause

- Modern investigations suggest that a combination of factors likely caused the Hindenburg fire. Static electricity, coupled with leaking hydrogen, is now considered the most plausible explanation.

- Advances in computer modeling and simulations have provided clearer insights into how the fire spread so rapidly, debunking earlier theories about sabotage or flammable paint as the primary culprits.

Progress in Aviation Safety

- The Hindenburg disaster accelerated the shift from airships to airplanes, prompting a reevaluation of how safety and reliability are integrated into the design and operation of new technologies.

- Today's aviation industry benefits from stringent international safety standards and advanced technologies that were unimaginable in the 1930s.

The Hindenburg's Place in Collective Memory

The Hindenburg disaster remains a potent symbol in the collective consciousness, representing both human ambition and the limits of technology.

Cultural Resonance

- The iconic photographs and Herbert Morrison's emotional radio broadcast—"Oh, the humanity!"—have immortalized the Hindenburg as one of history's most visually and emotionally impactful tragedies.

- The disaster has inspired books, documentaries, films, and artistic works, ensuring its place in cultural memory. These portrayals often emphasize the dramatic and human aspects of the tragedy, while modern historians strive to present a balanced perspective that includes its technical and historical significance.

Historical Context

- Modern perspectives often place the Hindenburg disaster in the broader context of 1930s geopolitics and technological evolution. The Zeppelin era represented a brief but remarkable chapter in aviation history, shaped by the ambitions and limitations of its time.

- The disaster also serves as a reminder of the interplay between technology and public perception. The Hindenburg's destruction marked the end of an era, not because airships were no longer viable, but because public confidence in their safety was irreparably shattered.

Ethical Implications and Modern Parallels

The Hindenburg disaster continues to spark discussions about ethics in technology and the responsibility of innovators to anticipate and mitigate risks.

Responsibility in Innovation

- Modern scholars often draw parallels between the Hindenburg disaster and contemporary challenges in fields like artificial intelligence, space exploration, and biotechnology. In each case, the balance between innovation and safety remains critical.

- The Hindenburg serves as a cautionary tale about the consequences of prioritizing economic or political factors over technical safety.

Resilience and Recovery

- The disaster also highlights the resilience of survivors and the aviation industry's ability to recover and innovate in the face of tragedy. These themes remain relevant in discussions about how societies adapt to disasters and use them as opportunities for growth and improvement.

Conclusion: A Tragedy with Timeless Lessons

From a modern perspective, the Hindenburg disaster is more than a historical event—it is a lens through which we can examine the challenges of progress, the importance of safety, and the resilience of the human spirit. While the Zeppelin era ended with the Hindenburg's destruction, the lessons it teaches continue to resonate in a world where innovation is often accompanied by risk. By studying this tragedy, we honor both the achievements and the sacrifices of those who sought to push the boundaries of what was possible.

CONCLUSION

LESSONS LEARNED AND THE END OF THE AIRSHIP ERA

The Hindenburg disaster of May 6, 1937, remains one of the most iconic and tragic moments in the history of aviation. Beyond the flames and smoke that consumed the world's largest airship lies a story of human ambition, technological innovation, and the stark reminder of the risks inherent in pushing the boundaries of what is possible.

The Hindenburg's Place in History

The Hindenburg was more than just an airship; it was a symbol of a rapidly changing world, one where technology promised to revolutionize travel, communication, and global connectivity. In its brief but impactful service, the

Hindenburg represented the pinnacle of airship engineering and the optimism of the early 20th century.

A Marvel of Its Time

- The Hindenburg's luxurious design and technological sophistication captured the imagination of the world. For a fleeting moment, it seemed to herald a new golden age of air travel, connecting continents with unprecedented speed and elegance.

- Its tragic end, however, marked the downfall of an era, as public confidence in airships evaporated almost as quickly as the hydrogen that fueled the flames.

Symbol of Ambition and Risk

The Hindenburg's story is a testament to humanity's unyielding desire to innovate and explore. It is also a cautionary tale about the consequences of underestimating risk, particularly in the pursuit of progress and prestige.

Lessons Learned from the Hindenburg Disaster

The disaster provided critical lessons that have shaped the evolution of transportation and technology.

The Importance of Safety

- The Hindenburg's reliance on hydrogen, a highly flammable gas, highlighted the dangers of prioritizing practicality and availability over safety. The lack of access to helium, due to geopolitical restrictions, forced the use of a more hazardous alternative, ultimately leading to disaster.

- This tragedy underscores the importance of rigorous safety measures and contingency planning in all technological endeavors, lessons that are now fundamental to modern aviation and engineering.

Public Perception and Trust

- The Hindenburg disaster demonstrated the fragility of public trust. While airships were once seen as the future of travel, the dramatic and public nature of the crash shattered confidence in the technology almost overnight.

- Today, industries recognize the critical role of public perception in determining the success or failure of new innovations, emphasizing transparency and safety to maintain trust.

The Role of Innovation in Crisis Recovery

- The Hindenburg disaster spurred the rapid advancement of alternative modes of transportation. In particular, airplanes benefited from the decline of airships, accelerating the development of safer, faster, and more reliable aviation technologies.

- This shift illustrates how innovation often arises from the ashes of failure, as industries adapt and improve in response to tragedy.

The End of the Airship Era

The Hindenburg disaster effectively marked the end of the Zeppelin era. Once a symbol of modernity and progress, airships became relics of a bygone time. The dominance of airplanes, with their ability to travel faster and farther without the risks associated with hydrogen, sealed the fate of airships as a viable means of commercial travel.

The Transition to Airplanes

- In the years following the disaster, airplanes gained prominence as the preferred mode of transatlantic travel. Advances in aerodynamics, materials, and engine technology allowed for safer and more efficient flights, meeting the demands of an increasingly interconnected world.

Lingering Legacy of Airships

- While the era of passenger-carrying Zeppelins ended, airships found new roles in niche applications such as surveillance, advertising, and scientific research. Their unique capabilities ensure that they remain a part of aviation history, even if their golden age has passed.

Reflections on the Hindenburg

The Hindenburg's legacy extends far beyond its tragic end. It serves as a reminder of the daring spirit that drives human progress, as well as the sobering realities that accompany innovation. The disaster resonates as a powerful lesson in balancing ambition with caution and has become a symbol of resilience and the enduring pursuit of excellence.

Honoring Those Who Were Lost

- The lives lost in the Hindenburg disaster deserve to be remembered, not just as victims of a tragedy but as participants in a bold experiment to expand the horizons of human capability.

- Memorials and ongoing historical research honor their memory and keep the lessons of the Hindenburg alive for future generations.

A Story That Continues to Inspire

- The Hindenburg remains a subject of fascination, appearing in literature, film, and art as a representation of both the triumphs and tragedies of human endeavor. Its story inspires continued reflection on the interplay between technology, risk, and the human desire to transcend boundaries.

The Broader Lessons for Aviation and Technology

The Hindenburg disaster transcends its immediate impact, offering lessons that have shaped not only aviation but also the broader landscape of technology and innovation. It serves as a critical case study in how ambition, risk, and technological advancement must be carefully balanced to ensure safety and public trust.

Lesson 1: The Primacy of Safety in Innovation

One of the most glaring takeaways from the Hindenburg disaster is the need for safety to be at the forefront of any technological breakthrough. While the Hindenburg was an engineering marvel, its reliance on hydrogen—an inherently flammable gas—highlighted a dangerous compromise made for practicality and availability.

Safety Over Expediency

- The decision to use hydrogen instead of helium, driven by geopolitical constraints, ultimately sealed the airship's fate. This emphasizes the importance of exploring safer alternatives, even if they are less convenient or more expensive.

- Modern aviation and technology industries have since adopted rigorous testing protocols and safety standards to prevent similar oversights. For example, today's aircraft undergo extensive simulations, stress tests, and fail-safe system implementations before being deemed airworthy.

Proactive Risk Assessment

- The Hindenburg tragedy underscores the need for proactive identification of potential risks during the design phase. Thorough risk assessments, combined with contingency planning, are essential to mitigate hazards and prevent disasters.

Lesson 2: Public Perception and Trust

The catastrophic nature of the Hindenburg disaster played out in real-time before a global audience, with photographs, eyewitness accounts, and Herbert Morrison's haunting radio broadcast. This immediate and visceral coverage shattered public trust in airship travel almost overnight.

Transparency and Communication

- The disaster revealed the critical importance of transparency in addressing public concerns about new technologies. A failure to clearly articulate safety measures or to respond effectively in the aftermath can have lasting consequences on public confidence.

- Today's aviation industry invests heavily in communicating its commitment to passenger safety through campaigns, certifications, and real-time updates during emergencies.

Media and Public Impact

- The Hindenburg's fiery end illustrated how media can amplify the perception of risk. This dynamic has become even more pronounced in the modern era of 24/7 news cycles and social media, where a single failure can undermine decades of progress.

- Organizations must be prepared to manage crises with swift, clear, and empathetic communication to maintain trust and credibility.

Lesson 3: Innovation Through Adversity

While the Hindenburg disaster marked the decline of airships as a dominant mode of travel, it also spurred rapid advancements in alternative technologies, particularly in aviation. The tragedy illustrated how failure can become a catalyst for progress when lessons are embraced and applied.

Shifting Focus to Airplanes

- The disaster accelerated the transition from airships to airplanes as the primary means of long-distance travel. Airplanes, which were faster, more versatile, and less reliant on volatile materials, became the focus of innovation and investment.

- This shift led to breakthroughs in aerodynamics, engine design, and materials science, laying the foundation for the modern aviation industry.

Iterative Improvement

- The lessons from the Hindenburg also demonstrated the value of iterative improvement in technology. Subsequent airship designs incorporated safer materials and refined engineering, even as the industry pivoted to other modes of transport.

Lesson 4: Ethical Responsibility in Technological Advancement

The Hindenburg disaster raises questions about the ethical responsibility of engineers, manufacturers, and governments in advancing new technologies. It serves as a reminder that the pursuit of progress must be tempered with accountability and a commitment to minimizing harm.

Balancing Innovation with Responsibility

- The German Zeppelin Company's ambition to create the largest and most luxurious airship highlighted the fine line between visionary progress and reckless risk-taking.

- Ethical considerations, such as prioritizing passenger safety and avoiding hazardous compromises, are now integral to the development of new technologies across industries.

Collaboration for Safer Innovation

- The geopolitical restrictions that limited access to helium played a significant role in the Hindenburg's reliance on hydrogen. This demonstrates the importance of international collaboration in addressing safety challenges and ensuring access to critical resources.

Lesson 5: The Need for Resilient Systems

The Hindenburg disaster exposed vulnerabilities in both the design and operational protocols of airship travel. Resilient systems—those capable of withstanding unexpected failures—are now a cornerstone of modern technology and aviation.

Fail-Safe Design Principles

- The concept of fail-safe systems, where a failure in one component does not lead to catastrophic outcomes, is a direct response to disasters like the Hindenburg.

- Redundancy, modularity, and the ability to isolate faults are now standard practices in engineering, ensuring that failures are contained and mitigated.

Continuous Monitoring and Adaptation

- Modern aircraft and vehicles are equipped with advanced monitoring systems that detect and respond to anomalies in real time, reducing the likelihood of disasters. This practice stems from a recognition of the importance of early detection and intervention.

Conclusion: Learning from the Hindenburg

The broader lessons of the Hindenburg disaster extend far beyond the world of airships. They resonate across all fields of innovation, highlighting the delicate balance between ambition and caution. By prioritizing safety, fostering public trust, embracing failure as a learning opportunity, and upholding ethical responsibility, industries can ensure that technological progress serves humanity rather than jeopardizes it.

The Hindenburg's story endures not just as a cautionary tale but as an enduring source of inspiration and guidance for innovators striving to build a safer, more resilient future.

Printed in Dunstable, United Kingdom